Working Together

Inter-school collaboration for special needs

**Ingrid Lunt, Jennifer Evans,
Brahm Norwich and Klaus Wedell**

David Fulton Publishers

London

David Fulton Publishers Ltd
2 Barbon Close, London WC1N 3JX

First published in Great Britain by
David Fulton Publishers 1994

British Library Cataloguing in Publication Data

A catalogue record for this book is available from the British Library

ISBN 1-85346-301-9

Designed by Almac Ltd., London
Typeset by Action Typesetting Limited, Gloucester
Printed in Great Britain by BPC Wheaton, Exeter

Contents

Foreword

The context

The past decade has seen a period of considerable change and development in the field of education and, particularly, in relation to the provision made for pupils with special educational needs (SEN). The decade spans the implementation of the 1981 Education Act in 1983, the 1988 Education Act and the 1993 Education Act. These three major pieces of legislation have led to enormous developments and changes in the way that LEAs and schools now provide education for pupils with special educational needs. The legislation has, in particular, raised questions as to where the responsibility for meeting special needs should lie. Following the 1981 Act LEAs took on more responsibility for providing for pupils with SEN, both through the statement procedure for the small minority with severe and complex needs (the so-called '2 per cent') and through other means of supporting a wider group of pupils with SEN (part of the so-called 18 per cent) in mainstream schools. The 1988 Act introduced Local Management of Schools (LMS) with the purpose of pushing back to schools the responsibility for a larger number of their pupils with SEN by the delegation of most of the education budget to individual schools and the retention of only a minimal resource centrally in the LEA. The 1993 Act and its accompanying Code of Practice and further LMS Circulars seek further to increase the responsibilities and the autonomy of schools by encouraging more schools to become grant-maintained, by specifying the nature and levels of support for SEN required to be provided by all ordinary schools and by further reducing the amount permitted to be retained centrally by LEAs. Further Circulars on 'pupils with problems' and on the organisation of special educational provision (DFE 1993c, d) specify other developments in provision to meet pupils' needs. It is in this context that this book presents the idea of clusters as one way of schools collaborating to meet pupils' special needs and thereby enhance their individual capacities to provide for these pupils.

The idea of clustering is not new. The literature reveals clusters in Third World projects (Bray 1987), clusters among small rural schools (Galton *et al.* 1991), and in Technical and Vocational Education Initiative (TVEI) projects. The formation of clusters of schools was one of the major proposals emanating from the Fish Report which considered the provision to meet SEN in the former ILEA (ILEA 1985). It was originally with a model of a cluster similar to that of the Fish Report that we began this research project to look at clusters as a form of collaborative arrangement to meet special educational needs. We were interested to study in detail cluster arrangements in LEAs which were linked to provision for pupils with special needs.

The book

The book falls into three parts. In the first part (Chapter 1) we aim to set the context for current considerations of provision for pupils with SEN. The context is one of turbulence and rapid change, yet in spite of this we believe that it is possible to develop initiatives which may enhance schools' abilities to meet SEN and indeed we have come across examples of these. In Chapter 2 we review some of the literature which describes cluster-type arrangements and which focuses on some of the factors influencing collaborative activity. The second part of the book reports on the research project carried out by the authors[1] and funded by ESRC through 1990–2[2]. The research involved a first phase of detailed case studies of cluster arrangements in four LEAs and a second phase of regional group discussions involving twelve further LEAs where there was either some form of collaborative arrangement in existence or under consideration by the LEA. It was immediately striking to see the wide range of collaborative arrangements existing in different LEAs; some of these different arrangements were referred to as 'clusters', though the word meant a different kind of arrangement in almost every case, while others were described as 'partnerships', 'consortia', 'families', 'academic councils' among other names. The case-study research was structured by a framework of cluster antecedents, cluster processes and cluster outcomes, and we attempted to relate factors within the LEA and schools prior to the formation of the cluster to factors in its operation and to outcome factors. This proved to be a complicated task, but we have identified a number of issues which appear to affect the operation and effectiveness of clusters. The third and final part of the book provides some guidance for schools or others who may be considering setting up collaborative arrangements. This draws both on the experience of this research project and on two of the authors' work in an earlier project which considered decision-making in relation to SEN (Evans *et al.* 1989).

Responsibility for special educational needs in the future

Current legislation and in particular the reorganisation of provision consequent on LMS has meant that a potential gap in provision has been highlighted. This gap concerns those pupils with SEN who 'fall between' the tiny minority of pupils with severe and complex needs for whom the LEA has to determine the provision by issuing a statement and the larger number of pupils with SEN who are the responsibility of the school but for whom the school perceives itself to be inadequate to provide. This 'gap' has been exacerbated by the reduction in central LEA services available to support pupils with SEN in mainstream schools and may be further widened by the requirements placed on schools of the 1993 Code of Practice. The task, therefore, for all schools will be to increase their capacity to meet the needs of a wide range of pupils and to enhance the nature of what is 'generally available' in mainstream schools.

Clusters, therefore, might provide a level between the LEA and the individual schools at which it could be meaningful and economical to organise some aspects of provision for pupils with SEN. This could provide schools with an opportunity to benefit from economies of scale and from sharing specialist expertise and equipment. For example, the schools of a cluster might fund a full-time support teacher to share time and expertise amongst the schools according to need, or a cluster of schools might pool resources for in-service training and more specialist equipment. A recently issued draft circular of the 1993 Education Act on the organisation of special educational provision (Department of Education 1993c) emphasises the importance and the benefits to be gained by schools consulting with each other, for example, to achieve economies of scale or to draw on each other's expertise.

In this book we present some of the ways in which schools have gained from collaborating in cluster-type groupings at the same time as presenting some of the potential demands made by collaboration.

The research has revealed fascinating aspects of the processes of inter-school collaboration and we hope to pass on some of what we have learned both to those who are interested to read about clusters and to those who wish to start up cluster arrangements themselves.

[1.] The authors were joined by Jane Steedman for part of the project. Her contribution is acknowledged.
[2.] The research was funded by ESRC as project ref. no. R-000-23-2571. The support of ESRC is gratefully acknowledged.

CHAPTER 1

The Context

Introduction

In this chapter, we consider the background to schools' attempts to meet the special educational needs (SEN) of their pupils from their own resources and those made available to them. The context in which this occurs is determined by the legislation on educational provision in this country, the principles underlying the legislation, and the ways in which all these work out in practice.

Background

The present context of schools' legal responsibilities for meeting their pupils' SEN derives mainly from the 1981 Education Act as now incorporated in the 1993 Act. The 1981 Act, which did not come into force until 1983, was itself based on the account of developments in the principles and practice of special needs education set out in the report of the Warnock Committee (DES 1978). The 1981 Act stated the qualified right of pupils with SEN to be educated in ordinary schools along with other children. The qualifications placed on this right were that this 'non-segregation' or 'inclusion' was compatible with:

- the wishes of the pupil's parents;
- the possibility of meeting the pupil's needs;
- meeting the needs of the other pupils with whom the pupil was being educated;
- the efficient use of resources.

The 1981 Act therefore set the stage for the basic question – how can the capacity of ordinary schools be enhanced to meet as wide a range of pupils' SEN as possible?

The Warnock Committee had asserted in its report, that children and young people's SEN occurred in a continuum of degree, and that it was not possible to draw a hard and fast line between pupils who could and could not be regarded as handicapped. The Committee stated that it was not useful to speak of 'handicapped' pupils, since handicap resulted from the interaction of factors within the child and factors within the environment. Consequently, from an educational point of view, the Committee felt that it was more relevant to speak of special educational needs, since this reflected the fact that pupils with disabilities and significant difficulties in learning might have a range of educational needs of various degrees of severity at different times in their education. It was in this context that the idea of a continuum of SEN came up. On the basis of several studies of the patterns of provision at the time, the Committee estimated that, while around 2 per cent of pupils were receiving their education in some specialist provision, a further 18 per cent received some form of special help at some time in their schooling – mostly in ordinary classes.

These kinds of considerations showed that one could regard the concept of SEN as applying to around 20 per cent of pupils, most of whom were being educated in ordinary schools. It was not, however, assumed that all pupils' SEN could be met with the resources available to ordinary schools. While the Committee felt that the 'continuum' of SEN should be met with a 'continuum' of provision, it was clear that the latter actually consisted of a variety of different resources ranging from those available to ordinary schools, to those only available in special schools and special units.

Dilemmas in providing for pupils' SEN

The scale of resources allocated to provision for pupils' SEN clearly depends, in the last resort, on how a community or a country decides to share out the funds available to it. It has been said that how resources are shared out in this context is the mark of a civilised society. Whatever the decision about the scale of the share, the question about how effectively the allocated resources are used still remains. Different degrees of SEN require teachers with different levels of specialist knowledge and skills, different specialist equipment and materials, and different environments for learning. Since the more severe forms of SEN are less prevalent, it is not cost-effective to provide for all forms of pupils' SEN in all schools. The different prevalence levels imply that provision has to be made with regard to economies of scale — and the most common way of dealing with this problem has been to concentrate resources for the most severe forms of SEN in special schools and special units, where pupils with those needs are then brought together in order to benefit from them. This creates the dilemma that meeting the requirement of economy of scale may run counter to the requirement for non-segregation of pupils — hence the conditions placed on the right to integrated education in the 1981 Act.

A second dilemma is implicitly related to the first. By setting up an organisational tier of provision above that offered by ordinary schools, almost inevitably a separate level of responsibility is established for pupils with SEN served by this tier. In this country, the responsibility for this tier of provision has rested with the Local Education Authority (LEA). These two levels of responsibility tend to operate in antithesis — the ordinary school may attempt to lean on the LEA for support in its more difficult tasks, while the LEA, in attempting to conserve its resources for the most severe forms of SEN, will wish to ensure that ordinary schools extend their efforts as far as is possible.

Different countries have sought to deal with these dilemmas in different ways (Wedell 1993a), often reflecting the different priorities of their societies in allocating their funds. Within this country, research has shown variations in the way that LEAs allocated the funding available to them (Goacher *et al.* 1988) and more recently, as we shall see later in this chapter, schools have been faced with new forms of these dilemmas, since they have been given greater responsibility in managing their own finances by the 1988 Act.

This then is the background to schools' strategies for enhancing their capacity to meet their pupils' SEN. The 1981 Act was formulated in terms of three ways in which pupils' SEN could be met. These comprised:

- the resources available in each school;
- the educational support services provided by the LEA (and the other statutory services such as health and social services and voluntary services) which schools could call on directly;
- resources which the LEA decided to make available through the Statement procedure either by allocating them to individual pupils in their ordinary schools or by moving the pupils to

wherever provision was made – in special schools or special units.

The Statement procedure

The current Statement procedure is derived from recommendations in the Warnock Report, but a procedure with similar purposes already existed previously. The details of the procedure took up the main part of the 1981 Act, and still does so in the corresponding part of the 1993 Act. There has been much confusion about the purposes of the Statement procedure and how it is intended to serve them (Norwich 1992). These problems were already found in research on the implementation of the 1981 Act (Goacher *et al*. 1988), and more recently were reiterated in a joint report of the Audit Commission and HMI (Audit Commission/ HMI 1992) and a report of the House of Commons Education Select Committee (1993).

The procedure was intended to provide a means whereby the LEA could justify allocating to an individual pupil resources which were not generally available to all schools (Wedell 1991). For this reason, the procedure involved an assessment of the degree and nature of a pupil's SEN by professionals from health, educational psychology, education and any other specialism felt appropriate. In the light of this assessment, the LEA could then decide the pupil's priority of access to specific resources and, if deemed appropriate, allocate them. This allocation was a semi-legal decision, and the 1981 Act provided for parents to be able to appeal if they disagreed. By the same token, the procedure also required the LEA to maintain the provision until such time as it was decided that the pupil's needs changed or ceased – in other words, the LEA was committing itself against itself. For this reason, the Statement procedure came to be thought of as 'giving the pupil the protection of a Statement'.

Quite erroneously, in some LEAs, the Statement procedure was only used where it was decided to place a pupil in a special school – in other words, where the provision involved both a degree of segregation and permanence of alternative educational provision. This seemed to indicate that the Statement procedure was regarded as a way of justifying the denial of a pupil's right to integration, rather than to justify the allocation of 'additional and different' provision (in the phraseology of the 1981 Act).

Whether or not LEAs maintained a Statement for a pupil was generally related directly to the level of support which they made available to schools. Research showed (Goacher *et al*. 1988) not surprisingly, that Statementing rates in urban LEAs tended to be lower than in rural LEAs, where it was less possible to achieve economies of scale in providing support to widely dispersed schools. In general, the proportion of pupils for whom LEAs maintained Statements tended to remain at around 2 per cent. This presumably reflected the commitment of LEAs to this proportion as a socially acceptable degree of need to qualify for additional individual resourcing.

There are two views about the variability in the proportion of pupils for whom LEAs maintain Statements. It can either be seen as a lack of clarity and consistency nationally in the expectations of the level of support which ordinary schools should offer pupils with SEN, or it can be seen as a consequence of differences in LEAs' plans for making provision. These two views follow from correspondingly different perceptions of the 1981 Act definition of SEN: 'a child has special educational needs if he has a learning difficulty which calls for special educational provision to be made for him'. The variation in the level of 'difficulty which calls for' may either be regarded as a lack of consistency or an acknowledgement of different approaches to the allocation of provision. The Audit Commission/HMI in their joint report (1992) regarded the variety of rates of Statementing as an undesirable state of affairs. One of the aims of the draft Code of Practice (Department for Education 1993b) specified by the 1993 Act (and discussed below) is to establish common criteria by which LEAs should decide when to maintain Statements.

Developments in provision following the 1981 Act

During the period following the publication of the Warnock Report and the coming into force of the 1981 Act, LEAs in general tended to allocate a higher proportion of their funds to meeting pupils' SEN, particularly in the development of support for pupils in ordinary schools (Goacher et al. 1988). There was a trend for pupils with all forms of SEN other than emotional and behavioural difficulties to be served in less segregated forms of provision than previously. Provision tended to be switched from special schools to units in ordinary schools, and from units to support in ordinary classrooms. Support in ordinary classrooms took the form of designated special needs staff in schools or LEA-based advisory teachers who both helped pupils directly and advised teachers about approaches for meeting the pupils' SEN (Moses et al. 1988). During the early half of the 1980s, ordinary schools were therefore increasingly able to call on the support which LEAs made available to schools.

Schools also organised themselves to provide a higher level of support. Although the 1981 Act was almost unique among comparable legislation in Western countries in promoting integration without allocating additional funds for achieving this, the government did decide to 'top-slice' training budgets allocated to LEAs, in order to be able to allocate central funds to train 'special needs coordinators' in ordinary schools. It was an innovative feature of the one-term courses set up to train these coordinators, that frequently the teachers were required, as part of the course, to make a contribution to developing 'whole-school policies' for meeting pupils' SEN (Cowne and Norwich 1987). HMI reported in 1989 (HMI 1989) that 50 per cent of primary schools and 25 per cent of secondary schools had formulated whole-school policies for SEN.

In spite of these considerable developments in the levels of schools' support, and of support which LEAs made available, there was still a gap between the pupils' SEN which fell within the 2 per cent level for which LEAs took responsibility, and the SEN which schools felt they could adequately meet from their own and generally available resources. This gap in provision became very apparent to the Fish Committee which, as was mentioned in the Introduction, was set up to review special educational needs provision in the former Inner London Education Authority, the largest LEA in the country at the time. The ILEA covered the twelve Inner London Local Authorities and was well known for the high level of support it provided for pupils with SEN.

The Fish Committee and clusters

In its report (ILEA 1985), the Fish Committee recommended that secondary schools and their feeder primary schools in a locality should form themselves into 'clusters' and collaborate in meeting their pupils' SEN by sharing resources. The Committee took the view that, by pooling resources in this way, ordinary schools could take joint responsibility for meeting greater levels of SEN among their pupils. More specifically, the Committee saw the function of clusters to be:

● the sharing of responsibility for most special educational needs which arise in the schools in the clusters and developing means of identifying and meeting them;

- providing a continuity of concern over the children's education in particular by facilitating close under-five and primary school links, and close secondary and tertiary education links in each cluster together with sensitive procedures for transfer from primary to secondary schools;
- to assist local decision-making about the forms of provision to meet SEN which are most appropriate for a group of schools and associated under-five and post-school arrangements.
- to provide a focus of service delivery so that members of all services advising and supporting schools and associated tertiary provision, including health and social services, can deploy staff to work with a small group of schools. Schools in their turn would be enabled to work with a known group of supporting professionals. (ILEA 1985)

The above means would not only enable schools to make better and more flexible use of the provision they had available, but, by forming themselves into clusters, it would become cost-effective for them to take responsibility for resources to meet more serious and less prevalent levels of SEN. By these means, the gap could begin to be closed between LEA-determined support and support provided on the initiative of schools and clusters of schools.

The Committee envisaged a hierarchy of levels of responsibility and services for meeting pupils' SEN, ranging from individual ordinary schools, through clusters, education divisions and groups of divisions, to the whole authority itself. These responsibilities and services would reflect the degrees of SEN and their relative prevalence levels, and consequently result in economies of scale and so achieve cost-effectiveness. Unfortunately, the ILEA was abolished by the government of the day before these developments could be put into place, although a start was made in some of the local divisions.

The Fish Report offered the most explicit promotion of the idea of grouping schools into clusters as a way of enhancing the level of SEN which they could meet, but similar developments were also occurring in a few other LEAs and in a variety of forms.

The impact of the 1988 Act

The 1988 Education Act (known officially as the Education Reform Act) had important consequences for the education of pupils with SEN, although initially it did not include reference to the range of education to meet special needs. The introduction of the National Curriculum, with its emphasis on the entitlement of all pupils, was widely welcomed as potentially enhancing schools' commitment to ensure access to a wider curriculum for pupils with SEN. However, it became apparent that implementing the National Curriculum, and the attendant assessment procedures placed enormous burdens of additional work on teachers (Dearing 1993), so that they had less time and energy to attend to pupils with SEN. At the same time, teachers became aware that the National Curriculum and the assessment procedures were very prescriptive, and reflected a questioning of their professional judgement, all of which resulted in a damaging lowering of morale (Dearing 1993). It was perhaps not surprising, therefore, that a steady rise occurred in the numbers of pupils referred for Statements, indicating a lowering of the level of SEN which individual schools found themselves able to meet (Evans and Lunt 1992).

The 1988 Act also introduced Local Management of Schools (LMS). In principle, this could have been beneficial for schools, because it gave them greater autonomy in managing their own finances, and so scope to respond more flexibly to their pupils' SEN. However, schools were forced into competition with each other, because their funding was allocated mainly on the basis of the number of their pupils, and because they were ranked on 'league' tables based on the aggregate performance of each schools' pupils in National Curriculum subjects. In the context of reduced funding, schools were then faced with conflicts if they allocated resources to pupils whose performance might not raise the aggregate achievement levels, even if, in principle, they had a commitment to do so. The general negative effect on school development of the introduction of league tables which do not recognise the amount of effort schools put into supporting their pupils, has recently been noted in the Dearing Report (1993), but its recommendations have not resulted in a complete abolition of league tables based on crude achievement levels. In the Audit Commission/HMI Report (1992), a survey is mentioned where 52 per cent of headteachers reported that they judged their funding to meet pupils' SEN as insufficient (although 69 per cent claimed that they were not limiting their admission of pupils with SEN).

The LMS regulations have also forced LEAs to delegate a higher proportion of their available funds to schools, and this has led to a systematic reduction in central LEA services to support schools at the same time as the schools have been experiencing difficulties in supporting pupils with SEN. However, even under these difficult circumstances, attempts to take positive action began to be made. LEAs started to develop formulae for allocating discretionary funds to schools, which took into account the extent of schools' need to support pupils with SEN (Lunt and Evans 1994). Systems of 'auditing' the proportions of pupils needing different levels of support have been devised, which are based on joint evaluations by LEA staff and the staff of the schools concerned. These evaluations are then used to share out the available funds. Some LEAs allocated funds to groups of schools, and left it to them to decide how the funds were to be shared between individual schools in the group. All of these approaches were intended to avoid the 'perverse incentive' which could result if funds were allocated on the basis solely of low achievement, whereby schools were not rewarded for taking action on behalf of pupils with SEN. These forms of auditing represented sophisticated attempts to match resourcing more closely to the continuum of pupils' SEN, and to schools' actions in meeting these. At present, some of these systems take considerable time and effort to administer, and it will be necessary to develop ways to avoid this while maintaining the aims of the audit. Unfortunately, the abolition of the link between LEAs' inspection and advisory roles, and the parallel alteration of HMI functions within the new Office for Standards in Education (OFSTED), has had the consequence that there is less scope for LEAs or HMI to support and develop the lessons gained from good practice.

The 1993 Education Act

The 1993 Education Act contributes both positive and negative factors to developing continuity in meeting the range of pupils' SEN. During its passage through parliament, a Special Educational Consortium (SEC) was formed of a whole range of bodies concerned with children and young people with SEN. As the Minister of State (Baroness Blatch) mentioned in the debate in the final stage of the Bill, the Consortium made a major contribution to the consideration of the special needs aspects of the Bill. However, the final version of the Bill which became the 1993 Act still fell far short of the specifications proposed by the Consortium. The Bill was reportedly the longest piece of legislation ever drawn up – it certainly required one of the largest numbers of amendments before it was enacted. Of the points relevant to the education of pupils with SEN, we will mention only a few of direct relevance.

A potentially positive feature of the Act is the inclusion of a Code of Practice which schools and LEAs will need to observe in meeting the range of pupils' SEN, both those with and without Statements. The Code requires all schools to draw up a whole-school policy for meeting pupils' needs, which will particularly cover the range of support which schools should offer pupils before a case for a Statement is considered. The governors of a school will be required to publish their policy and, among other conditions, they will have to report on who is the special needs coordinator and which staff have qualifications relevant to supporting pupils with SEN. These requirements have been further specified in Circulars on the organisation of special educational provision, issued for consultation shortly after the Code of Practice (DfE 1993d). All these requirements are to be monitored by the inspection teams visiting schools every four years. The Code thus places a responsibility on all schools to attend to these conditions, but, unfortunately, no indications are provided about how the measures are to be funded.

On the directly negative side, the 1993 Act fragments responsibility for meeting the SEN of pupils within an LEA area between the LEA and its schools, the grant-maintained (GM) schools and the Funding Agency for Schools (FAS) through which the GM schools will be funded. The Act prescribes three stages of change in responsibility – from the present situation, where the LEA has responsibility for all schools other than those which have opted out, to the point where 10 per cent of pupils are in GM schools, where the FAS shares responsibility for education within the LEA area, to the point where 75 per cent or more pupils are in GM schools, when the LEA retains responsibility only for those pupils who have Statements. Throughout the parliamentary consideration of the Bill, the SEC and others pointed out that this arrangement directly impeded the continuity of provision for pupils' SEN. The Conservative Chairman of the House of Commons Education Select Committee commented: 'If we really believe that SEN are going to be given a better deal under the new legislation than under the old system, then this is the biggest triumph of hope over experience that I have ever encountered' (*Times Educational Supplement* 1992). The government, in response, pointed out that its legislation called for mutual exchange of information between the LEA and its schools, the FAS and GM schools, about their special needs policies and, in the final stages of the discussion of the Bill, it brought in an amendment which called on the three parties to develop joint policies 'in so far as they were deemed necessary and desirable'. However, the comment quoted above can clearly be said to apply to this amendment also.

The 1993 Act is designed to encourage schools to opt out of LEA control and to place themselves under the control of the proposed FAS. The nature of the FAS's control is as yet unknown, but 'opting out' has been presented as a very attractive alternative for schools. Whether schools will regard it as desirable, if the switch ceases to be linked with additional funding, remains to be seen. It also remains to be seen whether opting out of LEA control leads schools to opt out of their responsibility to meet the educational needs of the pupils in their area.

There are plenty of indications that LEAs are having to scale down their centrally provided special needs support services to schools (Bangs 1993; Wedell 1993b, Fletcher-Campbell and Hall 1993). This is largely the result of the reduced funding which LEAs are permitted to hold centrally. Increasingly, this has led to the development of 'purchaser-provider' arrangements for the supply of support. As funds have been delegated to schools, it has been left to them to purchase support from existing LEA services, which, in turn, have been made to depend on such funding. In such an arrangement, it is left to individual schools to carry out their responsibility for the SEN of their pupils, by allocating their funds to such 'purchases'. Schools are, by definition, also free to buy support from other independently set up services. Similarly, in the case of a pupil with a Statement, the LEA may allocate the funds to cover the pupil's specified support to the school, and leave it to the school to buy the necessary services from wherever it wishes. The 1993 Act leaves the LEA with the responsibility to 'audit' the appropriateness of the school's use of the funds to meet the pupil's specified SEN. It is evident that the responsibilities for meeting a pupil's needs rest respectively with schools and the LEA as before. The argument put forward by the proponents of this 'purchaser-provider' arrangement is that it leads to greater accountability for the use of resources. The school can choose those support services which it is satisfied provide the support it requires. It is up to the remaining LEA services to ensure that they gear themselves up to achieve 'purchaser' satisfaction. Similarly, it is up to the LEA to carry out its 'auditing' function to ensure that the school provides the quality of support which a Statement specifies for a pupil.

The cold blast of market forces was regarded by the Audit Commission/HMI Report (1992) as what was required to ensure a more effective use of resources by LEAs and by schools. While many have agreed that greater concern for accountability would be beneficial in a time of constrained resources, it has also been pointed out that this does not have to be pursued in a way which risks disbanding precious specialist services. It is quite clear that a market-forces-led arrangement for individual schools, such as described above, makes quality services entirely vulnerable to the scope of schools acting on their own to be able – and willing – to afford them. In times of affluence, the risk of losing the services is probably slight. However, in the constrained financial circumstances of the foreseeable future, even those schools which have strong commitments to meeting the SEN of their pupils may be forced to cut down on the support which they are able to allocate to them. The schools will then either seek help from cheaper and probably less qualified personnel, or reduce their use of quality services. In either event, the revenue of services will be reduced, and will make them unviable. As the result of lobbying, these risks seem to have been partly recognised by the proponents of the 1993 Act, but the resulting amended section goes no further than permitting LEAs to continue to supply certain services centrally – specifically for 'low-prevalence' SEN according to a new Circular on LMS (DfE 1994).

Since the 1993 Act came into force, there has been an even greater awareness of the administrative problems entailed by its scaling down of LEA responsibilities. The National Commission on Education recognised the need for co-ordination at an LEA level, and proposed that local responsibility for education should be vested in Education and Training Boards (NCE 1993). In addition to the likelihood of administrative confusion, the need for co-ordination at local level also arises from the recognition that market forces do not, of themselves, generate obligations of responsibility to ensure the viability of essential support services for pupils with SEN.

Where next?

In the meantime, where are schools left with regard to the dilemmas mentioned earlier? The turbulence in the education system created by the recent legislation has certainly made it necessary for schools to face the choices surrounding their responsibility to meet their pupils' SEN. Clearly, the position of schools differs according to the proportion of pupils in opted-out schools in an LEA. In LEAs which have not reached the 10 per cent threshold, the situation for individual schools will not be as uncertain as in LEAs at the second or even third phase of implementing the 1993 Act. To some extent, the phase in which LEAs find themselves may reflect the nature of the relationship which they have with schools. However, the progressively increased requirement for delegated funding will affect the availability of all LEA support outside the Statement procedure. Also, although the government has acquiesced to the recommendation in the Dearing Interim Report (1993) that league tables should be abandoned at Key Stages 1 and 3, the impact of tables at Key Stage 2 and GCSE will still preoccupy schools with the need to compete for pupils. Schools will therefore still be faced with conflicts about the allocation of their resources. Schools will be more likely to look to the Statement procedure to supplement their funding for pupils with SEN, but LEAs will still be concerned to control their expenditure on Statemented pupils.

One of the aims of the Code of Practice is to clarify the respective responsibilities of schools and LEAs with regard to meeting pupils' SEN. In its draft form, the Code indicates that the expectations of schools' responsibilities to identify and meet pupils' SEN are greater than some may have anticipated. Schools' policies will need to cover a range of monitoring and support functions, which will entail a considerable amount of staff development for all teachers. The roles envisaged for special educational needs coordinators are substantial, and will require both training and significant time allocations. There is no doubt that observance of the Code will have considerable resource implications, and governors will need to review the priority they give to meeting pupils' SEN in their budgetary allocations.

The Code will also contribute to the criteria on which OFSTED inspections are based. The impact of inspections will, of course, depend on whether the inspection teams have the capacity to conceptualise the required standards and to evaluate the relevance of the practice they observe. The Dearing Interim Report supports the need to develop ways of evaluating schools on the 'added value' of the education they offer. However, the criterion of 'added value' itself needs to be carefully considered, to avoid schools feeling themselves constrained to achieve progress where it is achieved through least effort, and thus leaving out pupils whose SEN are less easy to meet. The Code will also form the basis on which schools will be called to account in any Tribunal procedures regarding appeals about provision to meet pupils' SEN.

It is in the broad context described above that forming clusters of schools to enhance their effectiveness in meeting pupils' SEN may come to be seen as offering a way forward. Collaboration may appeal more to primary schools, since their smaller size makes them more vulnerable. Secondary schools are often large enough to be able to fund a wider range of resources. However, they may wish to collaborate with their feeder primary schools, in order to help them in remediating the problems of pupils which would otherwise be passed on at transfer. Secondary schools will in any case be concerned to have good relations with primary schools which 'feed' them with pupils. If schools are concerned about the continued availability of educational support services which have been left to survive on the 'purchaser-provider' principle, they may look to establishing joint contracts between a number of schools with such services as a means of ensuring their viability. Where the co-ordinating responsibility of LEAs has been undermined by the proportion of schools which have opted out, schools may also feel the need to collaborate in their relationship with non-educational services needed by their pupils. The continued reorganisation faced by the health service will itself produce difficulties for schools requiring support, and it may be that schools will feel the need to collaborate in making their needs known.

Recently issued draft Circulars of the 1993 Education Act on the organisation of special educational provision (DfE 1993c) emphasise the importance of links and co-ordination between schools themselves and between schools and other bodies. Schools are required to explain in their policies their arrangements for working in partnership with other agencies and voluntary bodies. The draft Circular encourages schools to consult each other and to develop good links between SEN co-ordinators in an area in order to disseminate good practice and experience among schools for the benefit of pupils with special needs (DfE 1993c, para.77). The Circular suggests further that schools may wish to consult each other when arranging in-service training with a view to achieving economies of scale or sharing expertise. Cluster groups of schools could be one way of arranging such links and consultation.

It hardly has to be said that schools are currently finding themselves in a very difficult position. The same legislation which exposes them to the threats of competition also faces them with sanctions if they do not pay regard to pupils' SEN. Legislation also jeopardises both the educational and non-educational support services on which they have depended. The financial constraints limit both their own resources and the resources LEAs have to support the SEN of pupils. In the subsequent chapters of this book, we will examine the scope which collaboration offers schools and whether and how it has in fact been found to enhance schools' capacity to meet pupils' SEN.

CHAPTER 2

Principles of Collaboration

Introduction

Collaboration between schools can take many forms, from infrequent and short-lived interactions, such as course-work moderation, to long-term and intensive relationships, such as sharing staff or equipment. This chapter will focus both on collaborative processes in general and, specifically, on forms of collaboration between schools, how they emerge, what sustains or inhibits them, and what their advantages and disadvantages might be.

There are many terms used to describe collaboration, and all have different nuances and implications. Some of the most frequently used terms are: networks; partnerships; federations; links; clusters; consortia; and pyramids.

Networks

These are generally understood to be loose, informal, fairly widespread linkages between schools or between teachers in schools. Networks are often used for the exchange of ideas or for mutual support for particular groupings of teachers (for example, headteachers or subject teachers). The personal commitment of individuals to a network is not high: they join and leave as they find the need to. Networks of schools may work together on particular tasks (for example, an exhibition of pupils' work in the local library), but once a particular task is finished the network may disband. Networks serve to break down the isolation of schools or of individuals, but do not threaten the autonomy of schools.

Federations

At the other extreme, a federation is a permanent and extensive collaboration between a group of schools.

> Federation strictly implies the existence of some binding central authority circumscribing the individual autonomy of members. It properly describes schools merged under a single headteacher, but still on their original sites.
>
> (Benford 1988)

Federations are usually found in rural areas where a number of small primary schools are grouped together under one headteacher. With the advent of the National Curriculum and growing opposition to the closure of small village schools, federations are becoming increasingly common in some areas of the country. The 1993 Act has paved the way for small schools to opt out of local authority control by forming clusters with a joint governing body. One could foresee a development of this where the governing body might decide to group the schools under one headteacher.

Benford (1988) comments that federations of schools are common in Sweden and are not seen as a last resort to save non-viable schools, as they often are in Britain. Federations are resourced on the basis of commitment to the viability of all the participating schools:

> Thus there are many opportunities for an interflow of ideas and resources, exchanges of pupils and personnel, and a general broadening of experiences all round arising from a purpose-built system of management and provision in the first place ... In its most advanced form the model offers an exciting balance between individuality and the strengths of co-operation.
>
> (1988)

However, as Benford points out, schools may see the benefits of co-operation, but they would rarely recognise or desire a single unitary authority.

Clusters

Standing somewhere between the looseness of a network and the cohesiveness of a federation, one can find groupings known variously as clusters, partnerships, consortia or pyramids. Each of these terms may have slightly different connotations, but they share the characteristic of being, on the one hand, more formal and permanent in nature than networks, but less all-encompassing and controlling than federations.

For the purpose of our research, we defined a cluster as:

> a grouping of schools with a relatively stable and long-term commitment to share some resources and decision-making about an area of school activity. The arrangements are likely to involve a degree of formality such as regular meetings to plan and monitor this activity and some loss of autonomy through the need for negotiated decision-making.

It has to be said that many of the groupings that we came across in the research, while called clusters, did not fulfil all the criteria of our definition. For example, the schools were grouped for administrative purposes by the LEA and they shared some collaborative activities, such as INSET work, but that there was no loss of autonomy or commitment to share resources. However, as with federations, it was often in rural areas where the most extensive and committed clusters were to be found.

Clusters in rural areas

The concept of clustering schools has been extensively developed in rural areas, both in Britain and elsewhere. In this situation, the stimulus behind the formation of clusters seems to be the desire to increase resources in schools in rural areas. Bray (1987) writing about school clusters in the Third World, identifies the following purposes of cluster schemes:

Economic

- sharing of facilities
- sharing of staff
- bulk ordering of materials
- fostering community financial support

Pedagogic

- allowing schools to gain access to extra resources
- encouraging teacher development
- promoting curriculum development
- poviding an environment for innovation
- encouraging co-operation in school projects
- encouraging pupil competition (for example in sports and exams)
- integration of the different levels of schooling

- integration of schools with non-formal education

Administrative

- acting as a focal point to which instructions from higher levels may be sent
- acting as a centre for collection of information on enrolments, staffing etc.
- local decision-making for example on teacher posting and leave arrangements
- improved planning
- providing a better framework for teacher inspections.

Political

- raising consciousness about the causes of under-development and of the actions that can be taken by individuals and communities
- increased community participation in decision-making
- reduced regional and social inequalities.

(Bray 1987)

As can be seen from the above list, clusters in rural areas in the Third World have a wide range of purposes, some of which, at first sight, may not be applicable in a Western developed context. However, it is notable that many of the purposes of clusters can be applied to the situation of rural schools in Britain, including the administrative and political ones. The economic and pedagogic purposes are clearly similar. Small rural schools have much to gain from sharing facilities and staff, bulk ordering of materials and fund-raising within their communities. The pupils in rural schools will gain through access to extra resources and a wider peer group. There is also the opportunity for primary school pupils to become involved in a wider range of activities with a secondary school within a cluster.

The administrative tasks noted above may more usually have been carried out by the LEA, and some LEAs have grouped schools into clusters for these purposes. Since the role of LEAs has been greatly diminished by recent legislation (1988, 1992, 1993), there is less freedom for the LEA to influence the formation of clusters by schools. However, it may be that, in the future, the DfE or some regional authority (for example, the Funding Agency for Schools (FAS)) will find it useful to set up groupings of schools for some of the administrative purposes outlined above.

The political purposes of clusters are less overt in Britain than in Third World countries. However, there is the potential for groups of schools, with similar problems, to put pressure on LEAs or the government. For example, in one LEA which we studied, the governors of a group of inner city primary schools had formed a cluster to put pressure on the LEA to recognise the special problems of their schools and to allocate more resources. The potential of schools to opt out in clusters may increase the pressure that clusters of schools can bring to bear on LEAs or the FAS.

Government support for collaborative work

In 1985 the government recognised the need to enhance the curriculum in small rural primary schools and allocated funding through the Education Support Grant (ESG) to support collaboration between schools. An evaluation of the ESG programme has been carried out by at the University of Leicester by Galton *et al.* (1991). Between 1985 and 1991, fourteen LEAs received over £7 million to fund pilot projects to experiment in ways of enriching the curriculum in small rural primary schools. Many of these projects involved collaboration between schools:

> ESG funding was used to provide personnel, transport, meeting places and resources which were used to create, strengthen or extend:
>
> - contact and co-operation between neighbouring small schools
> - professional support groups of teachers, particularly early years teachers, and the exchange of educational ideas
> - classroom-based advisory support where previously advisory support had been minimal or non-existent
> - links between home and school, and links between primary and secondary schools
> - opportunities for children to work in larger peer groups; with more teachers than the two or three in their own school; ... and through the availability of a wider range of educational equipment.
> - involvement of governors and parents in their own local schools and in the schools nearby through joint social and educational events.
>
> (Galton *et al.* 1991)

Thus the clusters formed as a result of the ESG provided a stimulus for sharing of resources and expertise, breaking down the isolation between schools and teachers, enrichment of the curriculum for pupils, and the involvement of parents and governors.

Galton *et al.*'s extensive evaluation makes a number of important points about setting up and running clusters. In particular they point to the need to take a flexible approach to clustering and the use of support staffing across clusters to allow for differences between clusters and the stages of development that they have reached. The size of clusters is important. Galton *et al.* suggest that no more than six schools should form a cluster and that cluster groupings should not cut across other groupings in which schools might be involved. Training for those involved in co-ordination or support roles is necessary. This latter point is also made by Wallace (1988) in an article on management development in small primary schools. He makes the point that new heads of small rural schools are increasingly finding it necessary to collaborate with other heads and that not enough consideration is put into preparation for this task. Wallace's research indicated that heads found involvement in collaboration impinged on the following eight management task areas:

1. *Management policy:* developing a philosophy and school development plan which takes into account the views of other heads or support staff.
2. *Communication and decision-making structures:* involving outsiders in the school's decision-making procedures.
3. *Curriculum:* accepting the influence of outsiders in developing the curriculum.
4. *Staff:* fostering the development of mutual trust among teachers and support staff in different schools.
5. *Pupils:* ensuring compatibility of approaches among different schools to pastoral care and discipline.
6. *Material resources:* agreed procedures for procuring and sharing resources.
7. *External relations:* gaining the support of governors, including their acceptance of the legitimate influence of outsiders on the work of the school.
8. *Monitoring and evaluating the work of the school:* accepting monitoring and evaluation by outsiders.

(Wallace 1988)

These tasks, which heads perceived as necessary for successful collaboration, indicate some of the difficulties of achieving it and why, given the suggested benefits, there have been so few examples of successful clusters.

Problems in the way of collaboration

Hudson (1987) has reviewed the literature on inter-organisational behaviour and has provided a framework for the analysis of forms of collaboration. Although his analysis concerns a range of social welfare agencies, it none the less highlights some of the difficulties which may also prevent co-operation between schools.

> From an agency's viewpoint, collaborative activity raises two main difficulties. First, it loses some of its freedom to act independently, when it would prefer to maintain control over its domain and affairs. Second, it must invest scarce resources and energy in developing and maintaining relationships with other organisations, when the potential returns on this investment are often unclear and intangible. Hence it could be posited that an agency prefers *not* to become involved in inter-organisational relationships unless it is compelled to do so and that simple appeals to client well-being may constitute insufficient motivation.
>
> (Hudson 1987)

When considering collaboration between schools, particularly long-term and extensive collaboration, one can see that many schools would feel that, given the pressures they are under, the costs of collaboration would outweigh the benefits.

Hazenfield (1972) has made a distinction between 'people-processing' and 'people-changing' organisations. The former are engaged in placing clients in appropriate settings and therefore have an interest in setting up links with other organisations. Schools, for most of the time, are 'people-changing' organisations which are more concerned with operating within their own boundaries and are not, therefore, motivated to engage in collaborative activities. However, there are times when schools act as 'people-processing' organisations, particularly for pupils transferring from one stage of schooling to another. It is noticeable that links between primary and secondary schools for Years 6 and 7 are well developed in many areas. Indeed, clusters of schools based on links between a secondary and its feeder primary schools (sometimes called a pyramid or partnership) are one of the more common forms of collaborative arrangement. Apart from the need to collaborate over the transition of pupils from primary to secondary school, what other circumstances might induce schools to form clusters?

Hudson (1987) suggests that if organisations understand that they need to collaborate in order to realise their goals, then they will be motivated to do so. The extent to which schools are adept at forming relationships to obtain resources which might otherwise be unavailable to them could be seen as an indicator of organisational effectiveness (Yuchtman and Seashore 1967). Litwak and Hylton (1962) identify three modes of organisational co-existence each with implications for the likely development of collaboration: independence, inter-dependence and conflict. Two organisations may be said to be *independent* of one another if neither needs the other's resources to accomplish its goals and neither is interfering with the other's goal achievement. *Interdependence* may be said to exist when each organi-sation perceives that its own goals can be achieved most effectively with the assistance of the resources of others. *Conflict* arises when the goal achievement of one or more organisations occurs at the expense of others. Schools have multiple goals and may perceive that some of these (such as access to expensive equipment) could be achieved through collaboration, whereas others (such as achieving optimum pupil numbers) may necessitate conflict. At the root of collaboration or conflict, however, lies the question of access to and control over resources.

Hudson (1987) suggests that analysis of the ways in which collabo-rative activity develops involves three complementary approaches: analysis of the environmental context; the comparative properties of the organisations; and the collaborative mechanisms involved.

The environmental context

Hudson suggests that in 'turbulent' conditions organisations find it dif-ficult to survive on their own. Emery and Trist (1965) have identified the following indicators of turbulence: a large number of organisa-tions in the field (for example, surplus school places? competition between schools for pupils?); the inability of agencies to satisfy the demands for services (special needs provision? good exam results?); an unstable social situation (problems of inner city schools? school discipline and truancy?); a new programme piece of legislation (major legislative changes between 1980 and 1993 including LMS and the National Curriculum); and a retrenching economy (recession and cuts in public spending during the 1980s and 1990s). However, the existence of a turbulent environment, although threatening to schools, is not, of itself, enough to foster collaboration. Schools tend to be relatively closed organisations (Bell 1980). Thus, when they feel threatened, they tend to try to shut out parents and other interested parties. However, accountability and openness have become features of school management in recent years, and one might expect that confident and entrepreneurial schools may wish to collaborate with others if they perceive it to be to their advantage.

Comparative properties of schools

Schools that are similar in structure and intake may find it easier to collaborate than schools that are dissimilar. For example, a cluster which contains affluent suburban schools and relatively deprived inner urban schools may find it more difficult to organise joint programmes of activities, than a cluster in which the schools are relatively homogeneous. Large primary schools may not perceive it to their advantage to share their resources with small primary schools. We have already noted the distinction between people-processing and people-changing institutions which might account for the appearance of clusters based on a secondary school. It is to the advantage of a secondary school to become known to potential pupils and their parents. Thus, it may be motivated to share its resources with primary schools and to become a focus for collaborative work (see Weston and Barrett 1992).

Another aspect of the similarities or dissimilarities of schools and the likelihood of collaboration is what Hudson terms 'domain consensus'. That is, for collaboration to take place, there has to be agreement about the goals, philosophies and areas of expertise. Primary and secondary schools may differ on any of these areas, and therefore joint work may be difficult to achieve.

Network awareness is another prerequisite of collaboration. That is to say, schools must be aware of each other's potential contribution to a collaborative arrangement and see that there could be a possible matching of goals and resources that would result in a more effective achievement of those goals. Hudson adds that collaboration will also be affected by the extent of positive evaluation − the judgement by workers in one organisation of the value of the work of another organisation. Our research found one collaborative scheme which was not successful because of the negative evaluation of the secondary school by the primary schools in the cluster.

One of the key processes in any collaboration is that of 'exchange'. The concept of exchange implies that no goods or services are ever transferred without reciprocity of some kind being involved. Exchange analysis focuses on the power processes at work when organisations interact in this way.

> In exchange relationships, power is linked to dependence. It is precisely because the needs of *both* participating parties need to be fulfilled by an exchange (that is, it must be beneficial to both), that an integrated and rational system does not always evolve.
>
> (Hudson 1987)

Hudson goes on to say that an exchange relation is balanced when the actors have equal power, but that equality is not a precondition of exchange. What is necessary is that neither party is powerless in relation to the other. Inequalities in power (in terms of what one side might offer in a bargaining situation) may explain why very few clusters involve special schools in their arrangements. It might also explain why clusters which involve primary and secondary schools are often led by the secondary school. (It has more resources to bargain with and, therefore, takes a dominant role in any exchange.)

Another aspect of the resource/power issue is that secondary schools and larger primary schools will be less dependent on cluster exchanges for resources than small primary schools because the former control more resources and, therefore, have less motivation to join a cluster. In our research, we came across an example of a cluster where the larger schools would have preferred to opt out of the cluster, take their share of resources and manage them for themselves. They were prevented from doing this because the LEA's policy was to resource the cluster.

Types of collaborative linkages

Hudson argues that four key dimensions can be used for examining linkage mechanisms between organisations. These are: formalisation; intensity; reciprocity; and standardisation.

In terms of formalisation, arrangements can vary from formal agreements which have official sanction to informal tacit arrangements which often exist between organisations. The former are often 'top down', that is, they are mandated by the authorities who specify the terms of any collaboration. It has been suggested (Aldrich 1976) that such arrangements are often unbalanced in favour of one of the organisations and associated with lower perceived co-operation. This may be the case where LEAs have created clusters with insufficient consultation with the schools concerned, and which may cut across pre-existing informal collaborative arrangements.

Another example of formalisation is the existence of an intermediary body to act as a co-ordinator. Such a body can act as a facilitator or an inducer of collaboration. For example, in one of the LEAs we studied, a group of officers and advisers acted as consultants or facilitators to developing collaborative projects. This group also provided inducements to collaboration in the form of funding to groups of schools for their collaborative work.

The second dimension of collaborative linkages which can be studied is that of intensity. Aldrich (1979) identified two measures of intensity: firstly, the amount of resources involved in a relationship (for example, the number of teachers involved, the coverage of the collaboration in terms of pupils or subject areas or the cost of equipment to be shared); secondly, the frequency of the interaction. Some clusters have infrequent contact for the exchange of pupils or staff and thus their investment in the interchange is minimal. In other clusters, there is frequent and extensive interchange of staff, equipment and pupils. The more frequent and extensive a relationship between schools is, the more demanding on time and resources it becomes. Hudson (1987), therefore, suggests that, unless the success of a venture has been clearly established, organisations will be inclined to choose the less intense situation over one which is highly demanding.

The third dimension is the degree of reciprocity in the relationship (that is, the degree to which resources in the exchange flow in an equitable way between the participating schools). It is not necessary for the exchange to be symmetrical, but all parties must perceive that they are gaining something from it. For example, primary schools may gain access to facilities and equipment in a cluster with a secondary school. The secondary school may gain access to potential pupils and their parents. In a cluster of secondary schools, one or two schools may gain more resources (such as teacher time) than others in the cluster in the short term. However 'losing' schools may feel that, if, in the future, their needs grow, they would be able to draw more heavily on the resources of the cluster. This was the case in one of the clusters we studied. All the schools involved were willing to contribute, even though they may not, in any one year, have drawn out as much as they paid in.

The final dimension of collaboration which may be studied is that of standardisation. That is, the degree to which collaboration is influenced by whether or not what is exchanged is perceived as of similar value. For example, is the expertise and teaching experience of primary school teachers perceived as useful by secondary school teachers? Or is the use of a school minibus by outside groups seen as equivalent to access to school computers? Such evaluations need to be agreed if they are to be used as a long-term basis for exchange. If the units of exchange are similar (for example teaching hours or cash subscriptions) then it will be easier to come to agreements about them.

Strategies for achieving collaboration

Given the preceding analysis, strategies for achieving collaboration must focus on providing incentives for schools in terms of enhancing the resources at their disposal. The key appears to be that the costs of involvement in collaborative activities must be offset by gains for the organisation itself, either in terms of its educational goals or its survival as an organisation.

Benson (1975) calls this the 'political economy' of inter-organisational networks. He identifies three sources of pressure which might induce organisations to collaborate.

Co-operative strategies

This is trying to achieve collaboration through agreements and joint planning in which each organisation affected participates. This is a 'bottom up' strategy, where the schools themselves would decide to form a cluster. For such agreements to be successful, each school must hold something of value for the others and must be capable of resisting demands from the others. Such agreements are the outcome of a process of negotiation and bargaining during which each party agrees to the extent of resources to be shared and to the conditions placed on the use of the resources.

Incentives strategies

These constitute a purposeful attempt on the part of a higher authority (usually the LEA) to induce schools to engage in collaborative activities by making the deployment of extra resources conditional on joint projects or activities. Such strategies have been used extensively by central government in the case of TVEI and by LEAs to foster INSET work. In using such strategies, the authority can be prescriptive or permissive about the ways in which the clusters and their activities should operate.

That is, they can require certain schools form a cluster and they can lay down ground rules for cluster operation and the use of the funding or they can allow existing networks to form more permanent clusters and allow them to negotiate the use of the funding.

Authoritative strategies

It is less and less likely, under current legislation, that LEAs will be able to direct schools to form clusters. However, until recently, some LEAs have grouped schools into clusters for collaborative work or, more often, for administrative purposes. LEAs have found it useful for schools in a geographical area to be grouped for ease of communication and allocation of peripatetic staff. For example, a number of LEAs have formed clusters for the allocation of peripatetic special needs staff and educational psychologists. It is not the case that schools grouped in this way will engage in collaborative activities among themselves, particularly if there is no financial incentive to do so.

Collaboration for special educational needs

So far, in this chapter, we have been talking about clusters and collaboration in general terms, rather than how it might apply specifically to provision for special educational needs. Some of the more general points made earlier are thrown into particular relief when applied to special needs provision. For example, the objectives of clusters described by Bray (1987) included sharing of facilities and staff, encouraging teacher and curriculum development, integration across phases of schooling, simplified administration and increased community participation. Many of these are reflected in the Fish Committee's recommendation about the formation of clusters to support special needs provision (ILEA 1985).

As was pointed out in Chapter 1, the main point made by Fish was that increased delegation of responsibility for special needs provision was desirable, and that a group of schools within a geographical area (a cluster) should take responsibility for meeting the special needs of pupils in that area. Thus, Fish envisaged that clusters would consist of three secondary schools, their feeder primary schools and any associated under-fives and tertiary provision. Experience has shown that clusters of such a size are difficult to maintain as effective collaborative units.

The functions of clusters described in the Fish Report and presented on pp. 6–7 provide a useful basis for further consideration. What is missing from the list of functions from the Fish Report (ILEA 1985) is any notion of the delegation of resources to the cluster, without which the schools in clusters have no real power over planning or decision-making.

Many of the functions described in the Fish Report were present in the cluster arrangements we studied. Some of the more important seem to be: the concern for transition from primary to secondary schools; the usefulness of a cluster as an administrative unit for the deployment of outside services such as educational psychologists; an attempt to persuade schools to provide for a wider range of special needs within mainstream schools.

The original clusters concept from the Fish Report was further elaborated by Wedell (1986), who suggested that special schools and units could be incorporated into clusters to provide outreach work and a wider sharing of specialist resources. He also suggested that the resulting improved pattern of communication between services that he hoped would evolve from clusters should include parents, not only as recipients of support, but also as contributors to the planning of it.

It may be that, in these times of grant-maintained schools and local management of LEA schools (both special and ordinary), there will be more scope for the involvement of community representatives and parents in the planning of coherent patterns of provision for special educational needs. Certainly, the role of the LEA in planning provision will be severely curtailed under present legislation. The LEA still has a role as a facilitator and, by the way in which it deploys staff and funding, could provide the context for clusters of schools to plan and decide on the use of devolved resources.

A more recent elaboration of the cluster concept has been attempted by Gains (1992). He describes a cluster based on a school for children with moderate learning difficulties which also acts as a centre for the deployment of support staff into mainstream schools in the cluster. Schools within the cluster share the support staff time and other resources based at the centre. At present, the schools do not fund the centre themselves and therefore do not control the resources. But Gains envisages a time when schools will have more of the special needs budget delegated from the LEA and suggests that his model could be used as a way of providing economies of scale and ensuring a level of expertise which might not be available at the school level. He envisages that LEAs will be able to play an enabling role in setting up structures for support services based on clusters. However, as noted earlier, LEAs will need to be sensitive to existing networks of schools to ensure that clusters for special needs provision do not clash with other networks that schools have evolved and that they are responsive to their communities.

Conclusions

Schools are complex organisations with multiple goals and differing sizes, structures and contexts. They have been described as 'loosely coupled' (Corwin 1981, Weick 1976). That is, they are organisations within which the various elements are not tightly controlled from the centre, so that various groupings within the school, such as departments or teachers, can act independently from each other. Bell (1980) has characterised schools as 'anarchic organisations', by which he means that the goals of schools are unclear, that different members of staff may have differing goals or may place differing priorities to the same goals, or may even have difficulty in articulating goals which may lead to clear actions. Since 1980, the goals of schools have become even more complex and the tasks that schools are asked to undertake have become much more diffuse. Added to this, the environment in which schools operate has become more turbulent and impinges more on their work and life. Schools have been placed within an internal market, in which they compete for pupils and funding. They now have to be accountable for their performance to a wide constituency, which includes not only parents and potential parents, but also the wider community.

The new context of schools presents both opportunities and threats for collaboration (Hall and Wallace 1993). The new flexibility which schools have to use their funds could enable them to enter into collaborative arrangements more easily. However, heads would have to convince their governors and staff of the benefits to be gained. Also, there are limits to the amount of collaborative activity which could be sustained by a school, without detracting from its main mission with its own pupils.

Furthermore, within schools, special educational needs are not often a priority for the use of resources. Given the multiple goals of schools, there are often other areas where staff and governors would want to put their energies and resources. However, given what has been said earlier about making use of limited resources, and sharing scarce expertise, schools may come to see that their responsibilities for pupils with special needs could be more adequately discharged within a collaborative system of clusters.

The following two chapters discuss the forms which clusters might take and the ways in which clusters for special needs have been set up and run in a number of LEAs. The final chapter gives some suggestions about how schools might begin to explore the idea of setting up clusters in their areas.

CHAPTER 3

Types of Inter-school Collaboration

Introduction

In the research on which our book is based, we studied in some detail the setting up and operation of four clusters in four LEAs in England: two in the Home Counties, one in an outer London borough and one in an LEA in the northeast of England. We also gathered data on clusters in a further twelve English LEAs. The clusters studied differed markedly in their origins, structures, operation and objectives and the research revealed a range of very different kinds of inter-school collaboration. Although the research focused on inter-school collaboration in relation to special educational needs, many of the cluster arrangements had different goals and purposes. Some LEAs had a long tradition and culture of collaboration, and cluster arrangements there had developed and evolved within this ethos. Other LEAs were considering cluster organisation as a form of administrative arrangement in response to changes in education legislation proposed during the period that we were carrying out the research.

This chapter aims first to describe briefly the research which was carried out; it then attempts to characterise some of the different types of cluster which have been developed and which were encountered during the research. As shown in Chapter 2, a number of different collaborative arrangements have been described in the literature. During the course of the research, we became even more keenly aware of the considerable range and diversity of cluster arrangements being developed in LEAs, the term 'cluster' being used to refer to very different arrangements for groupings of schools, while other terms such as 'partnership', 'family', 'academic council', 'consortium' were also used to denote a collaborative arrangement similar to our 'cluster' model. Furthermore, many of the clustering arrangements that we encountered, particularly later on in the project, were experimental and provisional and often lacked clarity of objectives and functioning. This lack of clarity and formality was partly due to the general turbulence in the education system during the period of the research and the fact that LEAs were both adapting to the post-1988 Act context and developing their own LMS schemes and reviews of provision. This context has been described in Chapter 1.

As mentioned in Chapter 2 (p.17), we started out with a project definition of a 'cluster' denoting a relatively stable and long-term commitment among a group of schools to share some resources and decision-making about an area of school activity. It involved a degree of formality, with regular meetings of cluster schools to plan and monitor the activity. It also involved some commitment of resource (for example, teacher time) and some loss of autonomy, since a school had to negotiate some decisions in its area of activity. The cluster could be 'top down' (that is, LEA initiated) or 'bottom up' (initiated by the schools themselves), cross-phase or single-phase, concerned with special needs only or with a wider focus, and school managed or LEA managed.

The research

The research project involved two distinct phases. We wanted to look in some detail at the kinds of collaborative (cluster) arrangements existing among schools in a sample of LEAs, to study the processes by which clusters are set up and maintained, and to evaluate the effectiveness of a cluster approach to making provision for pupils with special educational needs. The first phase therefore consisted of four case studies of examples of cluster type arrangements. In the second phase, we wished to explore the idea of inter-school collaboration more widely and to take into account the opportunities and constraints of present and possible future scenarios in the education system. Regional meetings were held in different parts of the country to explore these issues.

The two phases of the research

In the first phase of the research, we had the opportunity to visit four LEAs and to carry out case studies. These involved the analysis of LEA and school documents and semi-structured interviews with appropriate key people at the five different levels of our interest: LEA (officers, educational psychologists, advisers, medical personnel if appropriate); cluster (co-ordinators, support services, educational psychologists); school (headteacher, SEN co-ordinator); classroom (class teacher); pupil. About 20–30 interviews were carried out in each LEA.

The second phase took the form of group discussions in three regions of the country. In each region we had invited representatives from four LEAs either where clusters were in operation or where they were under discussion, again seeking information from different practitioners, and thus learning about potential and existing collaborative arrangements in a further twelve LEAs.

The focus of the case-study research

We were interested in focusing our questions on the effects of cluster organisation at five levels: the LEA, the cluster, the school, the classroom and pupils. The research was structured across a time frame of (i) antecedents, (ii) processes and (iii) outcomes of the cluster. This meant that we asked questions concerning (i) the context in the LEA, the cluster and the school *before* the cluster was set up and factors which might have influenced both the decision to set up a cluster and the way in which it was set up, the *antecedents*; (ii) the early and current operation of the cluster and particularly the *processes* involved in running the cluster and the processes influencing its operation; and (iii) perceived *outcomes* of the cluster arrangement and reflections on its positive and negative results. We were also interested to hear from respondents about their views on the future, and about factors which might influence decisions on the part of the LEA, the cluster, the schools and teachers about the continuation or indeed the survival of the cluster arrangements. By structuring our interviews in this way, we hoped to gain a detailed understanding of the four cluster arrangements, their workings and the effects of this form of organisation on different levels of educational provision, in particular, that for pupils with SEN.

The case studies of four clusters

Although the idea of clusters has been well used in several areas (see Chapter 2) and widely discussed in relation to special needs following the Fish Report (ILEA 1985), when we came to identify our sample for the detailed studies, there were not many clusters to choose

from. However, by following up LEA contacts and placing notices
in relevant journals, we identified four LEAs which had some kind of
cluster arrangements and in which it was possible to carry out case
studies: Midshire LEA (Merestoke cluster), Northshire LEA (Seaton
cluster), Eastshire LEA (Oakridge cluster) and Southborough LEA
(Heathside cluster). Midshire is a semi-rural county which has a history of the LEA encouraging collaboration between schools. Northshire
is a county in the northeast of the country and Seaton cluster is in an
urban area well known for its close-knit community and the close contacts existing between its schools. The Oakridge cluster in Eastshire
is in an affluent semi-rural area of a large county. Southborough is
a London borough, again known for LEA encouragement of collaborative working. These four LEAs provided us with a range of different
forms of cluster organisation. A second group of LEAs was later identified for the second phase of group discussions through contacts in
the field of special needs provision.

The design and methodology for the case studies were derived from
the work of Huberman and Miles (1984). They developed a structured
approach to handling qualitative data to enable causal inferences to
be drawn in school evaluation studies, by collecting data over time and
attempting to link antecedent and process events with outcomes. We
adapted this methodology by developing semi-structured interviews
which were carried out with the key people as described above in the
four case-study LEAs. A common basic framework for all the interview schedules enabled us to use triangulation between respondents,
and we also referred to documentation received from the LEAs and
schools.

The following are examples of some of the questions:

(i)   antecedents: 'what concerns did people have which led to the idea
      of setting up a cluster?'
(ii) processes: 'can you tell me how the cluster is operating cur-
      rently?'
(iii) outcomes: 'have there been any specific changes in the ways in
      which schools relate to each other since the clusters have been
      set up?'

All the interviews were tape-recorded and transcribed and the tran-
scriptions coded according to a coding frame designed to provide
information according to antecedents, processes and outcomes, for
the different levels LEA, cluster, school, classroom and pupil. These

data were then sorted into code categories by a computer program designed to sort coded qualitative data. The ensuing analyses were subjected to progressive data reduction and final summary reports were sent to the relevant LEAs for verification and checking.

The group discussions

Group discussions were held in three regional locations, each involving invited representatives from four LEAs in the region. A 'focus groups' methodology (Morgan 1988) was used. This is a form of group interview which relies on interaction within the group through discussion of topics or themes provided by the researcher who acts as a moderator or facilitator. There were four such groups in each regional meeting. Each group of eight consisted of two representatives from each of four LEAs. The participants held a mixture of positions, for example education officer, adviser, educational psychologist, headteacher or governor.

The participants were briefed in advance with a short paper which described our definition of a cluster and stated that the aim of the discussion was to explore perceived benefits and the difficulties of operating clusters in the current and future climate in education. One member of the research team facilitated each group by ensuring that the discussions covered the participants' current experience of clusters; their reaction to the working model of a cluster used by the project team (see p. 17) and their views about the future. Since these group discussions took place at the time when proposed new legislation was being introduced and there was considerable turbulence in the education system as a whole, comments about the future and about the effects of the current situation on collaborative arrangements were inevitably somewhat speculative and hypothetical. We aimed to explore two different scenarios which might result from impending education legislation, one in which LEAs would continue to exist, the other in which LEAs would effectively cease to exist with widespread opting out by schools. We wanted to explore the different implications of these scenarios for collaborative arrangements in relation to special educational needs.

The group discussions were tape-recorded and subsequently analysed for themes and issues. The representatives were invited to a follow-up conference some months later at which we presented some of our main findings for verification and had further discussion of the implications of impending legislation.

In this chapter we consider some of the different forms of collaborative arrangements between schools studied in the research. Although it was not possible to draw up a systematic typology of clusters, we have identified some characteristics and features of the different cluster or collaborative arrangements. In Chapter 4, we consider in more detail some of the processes involved in setting up and running clusters and some of the outcomes of these forms of collaboration. We have already indicated that the word cluster is used to describe many different forms of collaborative arrangement and that other words are used to describe similar arrangements of schools grouping together for some purpose.

Descriptions of the four case studies

Cluster 1: Merestoke cluster, Midshire LEA

This cluster consisted of nine schools – one comprehensive and eight feeder primary schools in a rural area. Most of the primary schools were small village schools with teaching heads, although there were one or two larger primary schools in the cluster. Partnership between the schools was well established and valued. The LEA's policy over a number of years had been to encourage links between primary and secondary schools. These groupings of schools were called 'partnerships' to indicate that it was not expected that the secondary school should dominate the cluster but that there would be parity of esteem between the primary schools and the secondary.

Links between the schools were mainly concerned with the transition of pupils between primary and secondary, but also with sharing of resources and curriculum development. The schools in the Merestoke cluster had collaborated on a number of joint projects, which the LEA had set up to encourage collaboration. For example, a well-supported and well-funded project on curriculum enhancement designed to raise levels of achievement was coming to an end as we started our research in the cluster.

The project we studied involved the secondary school and four of the eight primary schools. The secondary school had invited those particular schools to participate because they had not been involved in the previous curriculum enhancement project. The collaboration was concerned with behaviour management and the aim was to achieve a common approach across the schools. The project was financed by GEST (Grants for Education Support and Training) for work on the Elton Report. The government had given a high priority to development work in schools for the purpose of implementing the recommendations of the report of the Elton Committee (Discipline in Schools 1989). The LEA was keen to develop the partnerships and, when it received a GEST grant for work on behaviour and discipline in schools, it decided to ask groups of schools within the partnerships to bid for funds to work on projects concerned with behaviour. Thus the group of schools we studied had been working together over a period of a year on developing a partnership approach to behaviour and discipline. This had involved teachers from the primary and the secondary schools visiting each others' schools and observing classroom behaviour and its management. The co-ordinating group, which consisted of the heads of the primary schools (which were small rural schools) and a senior teacher from the secondary school developed and ran an in-service day for all teachers in the partnership's schools. This day was designed to begin the process of developing a partnership policy on behaviour. The LEA monitored the project, but left the day-to-day running to the schools themselves.

A strong partnership identity had emerged, as a consequence of this work, to the extent that the heads of some of the primary schools involved were wanting to drop their links with another (single-phase) grouping to which they belonged, which consisted of a different set of schools (some of which were in the partnership and some not) and concentrate their collaborative efforts on the partnership.

Cluster 2: Seaton Cluster, Northshire LEA

This cluster consisted of six secondary schools in an urban area in the northeast. The cluster was concerned with support for schools in the management of difficult behaviour. The cluster was initiated and managed by the heads of five of the six comprehensive schools in one town, along with the senior educational psychologist. The sixth school, which had initially decided not to participate, joined the cluster at a later date. The collaboration was originally conceived as a method of providing an off-site unit to be used by the schools, but quickly developed into a support team which worked with pupils with behaviour problems in their schools, rather than as an off-site facility to which disruptive pupils would be sent.

The resources shared and managed by the group of heads consisted, until recently, of a full-time team leader and a number of part-time team members who were seconded from the staff of the schools concerned. The full-time team leader was funded by the LEA, but managed by the heads. The size of the full-time team was later increased to four and the management of these staff is now shared between a county head of service and the heads.

Each head would decide how much teacher time was to be put into the team (usually 0.2 or 0.3 fte) and allocation of support to the schools was on the basis of their current need for support, rather than on the amount of time each contributed. The teachers, who were seconded for one or more years, would receive training from the team leader in methods of supporting pupils with behaviour difficulties and would be allocated to support pupils in schools other than their seconding school. Pupils whose behaviour was causing concern were referred by the schools to the team leader who would allocate support time.

A rotation of staff, with individual teachers serving on the team for two or three years in the main, meant that the cluster served a staff development function as well as a support role, in that, over the years, a number of teachers from the schools received the training and experience of working in the team. These teachers were enabled to take the expertise they had gained back into their schools and, in many cases, had gained promotion as a result.

In this cluster, the sharing of resources and joint management of staff brings it closest to the model which we had developed to describe a cluster. That is to say, the collaboration involved some sharing of resources and expertise.

Cluster 3: Oakridge Cluster, Eastshire LEA

Eastshire LEA had set up clusters of primary schools in order to form administrative units for SEN in each of the six LEA local areas. These units were serviced by a team of administrators based in the area offices. The decentralisation of the management of SEN resources to local area offices was part of a strategy within the LEA to make areas more self-sufficient as far as SEN were concerned and to make services more responsive to local needs and existing provision.

Oakridge was a cluster of about 25 primary schools in an affluent semi-rural area. The clusters within each local area were formed from groups of schools which had been supported by a remedial reading service based on the site of a primary school within each cluster. The reading service had been transformed from a withdrawal service, to which pupils were sent to receive extra help with reading problems, into an integrated support service, which worked within schools supporting and advising teachers as well as supporting pupils.

The support teachers for SEN were deployed on a cluster basis, as were, as far as possible, health services and education social workers. As far as allocating SEN resources was concerned, the cluster was the location of a twice-termly meeting of a multi-disciplinary team which received requests from the schools for extra resources for children with SEN. It was, in effect, a panel meeting. Individual schools would send representatives to the meeting, who would come before the panel at a designated time to put the case for their school.

Cluster meetings were, therefore, multi-disciplinary case conferences on individual children put forward for consideration by schools. Resources were not shared within the cluster − they were allocated by the central team which consisted of health, social services, education social workers, psychologists, education officers and support service co-ordinators. There was, therefore, no sense of a cluster identity among the schools as far as planning or allocating resources for SEN was concerned. The schools themselves did not meet as a cluster.

Cluster 4: Heathside Cluster, Southborough LEA

Southborough LEA has established several geographical and administrative divisions, which it has called clusters, for transition between phases of schooling, each consisting of a mainstream secondary school and its associated first and middle schools. The patterns of transition within the borough and the siting of the comprehensive schools made it possible for six well-defined clusters to be set up. Provision for SEN was not part of the original conception of cluster activity, but became a feature of the arrangements as the clusters developed and SEN staff within the LEA saw the potential of the clusters to provide a more coherent arrangement for SEN provision and to advance the borough's policy of providing for SEN within mainstream schools in the borough.

Nine schools made up the Heathside cluster − one comprehensive and eight feeder first and middle schools in a relatively affluent urban area. Within the cluster the comprehensive school and two of the first and middle schools were additionally resourced − that is, they were equipped to provide for children with physical impairment and for children with moderate learning difficulties. The additional resources deployed into the schools consisted of one full-time teacher and one full-time classroom assistant. The additionally resourced schools did

Table 3.1 The four case-study clusters

	Origin	Size	Phase	Purpose	Management
Cluster 1	Top down	9 schools	Cross-phase	Behaviour and transition	Schools
Cluster 2	Bottom up	6 schools	Secondary	Behaviour	Schools
Cluster 3	Top down	25 schools	Primary	SENs resource allocation	Area office
Cluster 4	Top down	9 schools	Cross-phase	SENs resource allocation and transition	LEA central admin

not act as a resource for the other cluster schools. Their role was to make provision for up to ten children from within the cluster catchment area who had Statements.

The Southborough clusters were also used by the LEA as a means of systematising the deployment of SEN resources. Support teachers were organised on a cluster basis, as was the educational psychology service. There had been an intention to delegate control of some SEN provision to the cluster, which would take responsibility for its deployment, but this had not yet happened. Thus the potential of clusters to promote collaboration between schools had not been fully realised. The primary schools' main links were with the secondary school and focused on transition for all their pupils. There was very little joint activity concerned with special educational needs between the primary schools or between primary and secondary schools.

Table 3.1 summarises some of the characteristics of the four clusters which were studied in detail through the case studies. These descriptive characteristics of the clusters will be discussed in terms of some of the dimensions on which clusters differ.

Some of the arrangements described during the focus group meetings

It is not possible to present in detail the range of collaborative arrangements which were taking place in the twelve LEAs which

Table 3.2 Cluster types from the regional group discussions

	Origin (School or LEA)	Size (no of schools)	Phase	SENs provision	Funding source
Cluster 5	mixture	7 – 10 schools	cross-phase	non-Statement	schools
Cluster 6	mixture	11 schools	cross-phase (and special)	non-Statement	LEA and schools
Cluster 7	LEA	5 – 9 schools	primary	non-Statement	LEA
Cluster 8	both	5 – 20	cross-phase	n/a	n/a
Cluster 9	LEA	ave 6/7	cross-phase	non-Statement	LEA
Cluster 10	LEA	5	cross-phase	non-Statement	LEA
Cluster 11	LEA	24	cross-phase	n/a	n/a
Cluster 12	LEA	16	primary	non-Statement	LEA

were involved in the regional group discussions. However, it was clear that in almost all of these LEAs (which had been chosen for this reason) there was some form of collaboration between schools and that this usually involved SEN. Features of these groupings of schools will be included in the discussion of the dimensions of clusters. Table 3.2 presents some of the features of some of the cluster arrangements which were described in the regional meetings, though it was not possible to create a detailed summary typology of all 12 cluster groupings described. It quickly became apparent from the research that each cluster arrangement was both unique, and very complex and dependent on very specific local circumstances and personnel.

Dimensions for describing inter-school collaboration

We have attempted here to consider the following dimensions of cluster arrangements, giving some examples and considering some of the advantages and disadvantages involved:

- initiation/origin;
- phase and type of schools involved;
- extent of collaboration;
- focus/purpose of collaboration;
- source of funding;
- nature of SEN provision.

Origin

We drew the distinction between 'top down' (LEA-originated) and 'bottom up' (schools-initiated) origin of clusters. It became clear that the majority of the clusters concerned with special educational needs were initiated 'top down' by the LEA. In some cases, this was as a form of administrative structure or tier for the allocation of additional resources (as in the Oakridge cluster of Eastshire). In the Heathside cluster in Southborough, also initiated by the LEA, additional resources were allocated to three of the schools which received children with special needs from other schools in the cluster; however, in both of these clusters there was very little collaboration between the schools themselves.

In Midshire LEA, GEST funding enabled the LEA to fund schools to collaborate over a specific initiative. Other 'top down' cluster arrangements formed part of an LEA strategy for planning post-1988 Act and, in particular, in relation to LMS; for clusters concerned with special needs, this might form part of the LEA's strategy to deal with the increase in the demand for Statements and to introduce more accountability and clarity of responsibility in relation to resourcing for SEN. Circular 7/91 had produced the need for greater planning and accountability for SEN resourcing, while the effects of the 1988 Act and LMS in particular had led in many LEAs to a considerable increase in the demands for Statements. Two LEAs delegated SEN resources to cluster groups of schools in order to increase local responsibility and decision-making in relation to SEN and to reduce demand for Statements. Resources had to be accessed through the group which held regular meetings to decide on the priorities of its different schools.

In another LEA, the cluster would bid for additional central resources from the LEA to meet the needs of the cluster schools, thus involving a considerable degree of joint cluster decision-making. Some LEAs from which we gathered data in the regional group discussions were considering some form of cluster organisation in their

SEN reviews, both as a means of devolving resources to a level below the LEA and in order to introduce some process of moderation or awareness raising in relation to schools' demands for additional resources. For some LEAs, there was a realisation that a cluster of schools could give a sufficiently large pupil population for level of need across the population to remain fairly constant from year to year thus facilitating planning and resource allocation. In some LEAs, therefore, there was an intention to devolve responsibility and resources for SEN to the level of the cluster in order to increase local ownership and therefore responsibility and also to make clear the finite nature of SEN resources. There was a hope that collaboration between schools could help schools to realise the relativity and shared nature of their problems and the fact that resources for SEN were finite and required decisions for prioritising needs.

Although, in theory at least, clusters might be initiated by schools themselves, 'bottom up' as opposed to 'top down' by the LEA, we saw few examples of this. This was perhaps because, at the time we carried out the case studies, additional resources for SEN were still generally retained by the LEA and allocated by them. However, the Seaton cluster in Northshire provided one example of 'bottom up' initiation, although its existence was also later facilitated by LEA involvement. In another LEA, less formalised and more 'organic' development groups had developed which were said to focus on the schools' own concerns; these groups had tended to involve shared meetings, though no formalised sharing of resources.

Some clusters appeared to have been initiated by the LEA almost in partnership with the schools. In one example, two comprehensives, eight primary schools and a special school collaborated originally with their delegated INSET budget and subsequently for SEN, receiving a budget from the LEA which they supplemented by a proportion from their own budgets.

Whether a cluster is initiated by the LEA or the schools themselves or a partnership of the two depends in part on the function intended for the cluster. At a time when the LEA has more power over resources, it is easier for the LEA to initiate cluster arrangements and to define and control their purpose and functioning. LEA-originated clusters have been used for two distinct kinds of purposes, either to foster collaboration between schools or as an administrative tier for the delegation of resources for SEN. On the other hand, when schools have more control over their own resources it may be easier for them to initiate collaboration in order to achieve particular goals. Clusters may in this case achieve economies of scale, professional support and sharing of expertise or opportunities for staff development.

In the wake of the 1993 Act and the considerably weakened powers of LEAs, it may be that we are moving towards a situation where, in order to survive and to be of any significance, clusters will need to develop from the schools themselves more organically rather than being formed as administrative structures by LEAs.

Phase and type of school

Some clusters take the form of 'pyramids' of schools, a comprehensive and its feeder primary schools, sometimes, but by no means necessarily, including a special school. This was the kind of cluster envisaged by the Fish Report (ILEA 1985) in which a community would be served by a cluster of schools collaborating to meet the SEN of the children and young people in the community. We found several examples of 'pyramid' clusters whose main concern was transition but which also involved some special needs element. Both Midshire and Southborough case studies provided examples of 'pyramid' clusters and in both of these the secondary school played a major and leading role. Neither of these clusters involved a special school.

In clusters where the 'pyramid' included a special school, this might serve as a resource centre for the cluster; one example of this involved considerable outreach work which made it possible to further the integration of pupils into local mainstream schools. Another cluster arrangement, originally based on INSET, involved two comprehensive schools putting in 10 per cent of their delegated INSET budget and the local primary schools and a special school putting in 25 per cent of their budget to appoint a co-ordinator to serve the group of schools. The INSET focus had been extended to include special needs and the cluster experienced a strong sense of 'cluster' identity.

Other clusters were single phase, usually, but not always, involving a group of primary schools. Eastshire provided an example of a primary cluster though it involved little active collaboration between the schools themselves. It did, however, serve as a forum to consider the SEN of pupils in the group of primary schools. Another LEA had clusters of eight to ten primary schools grouped together mainly for INSET purposes, which involved planning meetings and sharing of some resources. In two LEAs, we encountered primary schools which were additionally resourced and which were originally intended to take the pupils with SEN from other primary schools in the local cluster.

One of these LEAs gave additional resources to a primary school in each cluster to take pupils with moderate learning difficulties from the schools of the cluster, the aim being to obviate the need for Statements and to enable economies of scale. Northshire involved a group of secondary schools which collaborated very actively and whose parity of status and concerns may have made collaboration easier for them than if they had involved primary schools as well.

However, the question does arise whether transition clusters may inhibit true mutual collaboration because of the perceived and actual power and resource differences between primary and secondary schools and their differing concerns in relation to special needs resultant from formula funding and open enrolment. In several transition clusters the secondary school played a leading and dominant role; however, this role may change as a result of the pressures of open enrolment and competition for pupils. This question was raised in the group discussions, particularly since some secondary schools were perceived to have less need for collaboration since they had substantial delegated resources of their own. On the other hand, it was also pointed out both that good relationships and collaboration with local primary schools were important because of open enrolment and that today's children with SEN in primary schools would be tomorrow's pupils in the secondary school. One secondary headteacher considered that it was possible and even prudent to be altruistic, since sharing resources for SEN with primary schools might prove to be an investment in future pupils if their SEN could be met earlier.

It may be easier to develop active and participative collaboration amongst single-phase groups of schools where there is greater parity of status, comparative similarity of resources and mutuality of concerns, than in groups involving both primary and secondary schools. The advantages to such clusters were apparent during the course of the study. Special educational needs is an area where competitiveness and market forces may have less significance and therefore be less detrimental to collaboration between schools, though it may be easier to see the immediate mutual benefits for single-phase groups of schools than for pyramids.

Extent of collaboration

As is already evident, clusters differed in the extent and nature of their collaboration. The original definition of 'clusters' used by the project implied an active collaboration and included a commitment of resource and some loss of autonomy. However, it immediately became evident that by no means all of the cluster arrangements encountered necessitated active or indeed any collaboration. The word could also simply mean grouping. At one end of this continuum were cluster arrangements involving schools either in active collaboration or in sharing and pooling some of their own resources or in both. At the other end of the continuum of collaboration were clusters which existed as administrative arrangements but in which the schools played little or no active part and which involved no collaboration amongst the schools themselves; the cluster existed as a form of administrative structure used by the LEA as an intermediate level between LEA and schools.

The extent of collaborative arrangements depended partly on where responsibility for pupils with SEN was felt to be located or who had responsibility for these pupils. In cluster arrangements used by the LEA to allocate resources and which involved no collaboration between the schools (for example, Eastshire LEA), the LEA retained responsibility and the cluster might serve as some form of moderation or filter to determine more equitable allocation of resources from a finite budget. In Eastshire the cluster operated as a multi-professional forum for a group of schools to gain access to additional resources for SEN. The schools themselves did not have to collaborate or communicate with each other.

On the other hand, arrangements were found in which the LEA made additional resources contingent on collaboration, for example in Midshire, where the schools had to present their plan for collaboration in order to gain access to the extra resources. In another cluster, the schools themselves took some responsibility for the SEN of pupils within the cluster and had resources delegated to meet these needs, often by a teacher being allocated to the cluster and sharing her time between the schools of the cluster. One LEA, for example, allocated support teams of teachers and non-teaching assistants to the cluster to be deployed by the cluster according to the perceived needs of the schools involved. Such an arrangement involved considerable collaboration and negotiation between the schools. These arrangements shifted some responsibility for pupils with special needs on to the schools themselves, although this was facilitated by the LEA's resources.

Finally, at the other end of this continuum, Northshire provided an example of a group of schools which collaborated actively, pooled some resources (teacher time) and received additional resources to the cluster from the LEA. In this way they were able to retain responsibility for a larger number of pupils with SEN (behaviour problems in this case) and to support each other in so doing. This cluster necessitated considerable negotiation, some loss of autonomy for the individual schools and some joint planning and decision-making.

It could be suggested that the incentive for schools to collaborate by pooling resources only exists in so far as they feel a responsibility for pupils with SEN. The report by the Audit Commission (1992) recommended that the respective responsibilities of LEA and schools be clarified. The implication is that with a reduced LEA and its support services and with increased delegation for SEN to schools, schools themselves will have responsibility for all but the tiny minority of pupils with very severe and complex special needs. In this case, where schools have responsibility for meeting the needs of virtually all pupils, there may be an incentive to pool resources in order both to achieve economies of scale and to develop different forms of support within a cluster. Clearly the extent of collaboration is and will be influenced by the extent to which schools feel responsibility and the extent to which they consider that the advantages and benefits of collaboration outweigh the disadvantages and costs.

Focus of collaboration

In many instances, clusters for special educational needs exist as part of groupings for other purposes, either as extensions of them or as parallel add-ons. Many cluster groupings have been set up either for transition, National Curriculum or curriculum enrichment. This form of grouping has been used extensively in some LEAs for small rural schools in order to counter some of the effects of size and isolation. In other cases clusters started through TVEI, for example, and then took on some SEN focus at a later stage. In some LEAs different cluster groupings exist for different purposes and in some cases the fact that these groupings are not co-terminous may have led to some confusion and lack of commitment.

However, as already noted, several LEAs had created cluster arrangements specifically for SEN as part of their review of special education provision, either as a means for allocating resources from a finite budget or as a means of achieving economies of scale or both. For these LEAs the focus on SEN meant that the nature and scope of the collaboration may have been clearer than for those with a more general collaboration focus. The clusters in Northshire and Midshire had an even more specific and indeed limited focus within special needs and may thus have been more straightforward to manage through this limited task focus. This issue will be discussed further in Chapter 4.

Collaboration clearly involves time and is dependent on developing relationships between the professionals involved. Schools themselves are highly complex organisations and it is a complex task to collaborate with other schools. From the clusters encountered, there is evidence to suggest that a specific focus is needed in order to facilitate collaboration and that collaboration *per se*, although often acknowledged to be of benefit, may be too complex and difficult to maintain without a specific focus or at least a specific person who is committed to the development and maintenance of collaboration.

Source of funding

Cluster resources may come from either the LEA or the schools from their own budget or from both. Cluster resources for SEN may take the form of resources delegated to the group of schools by the LEA as additional resources for pupils with SEN or of resources pooled by the schools from their own budget to enhance their own provision or support. It was possible to trace a continuum of resourcing amongst the clusters studied. At one end, schools might pool some of their own resources. In other cases, schools might pool some of their own resources which were then added to by the LEA. A group of schools might manage the resources delegated to it by the LEA. Or one school in the cluster might be additionally resourced and thus manage the additional resource from the LEA.

Clearly, clusters originated and managed by the LEA are likely to be also resourced by the LEA, for example as part of an integration policy or as part of its delegation to schools. In these cases the LEA may use the cluster as part of its SEN policy in order to further integration and to increase the schools' sense of ownership and responsibility for the pupils within their community or locality who have special educational needs. As has already been mentioned, some LEAs were using the cluster as a level for delegating SEN resources as part of LMS. This enabled some LEAs to indicate the extent and the finite nature of the additional resources and to pass over to the schools the task of allocating resources to individual schools according to different need. This form of delegation may also have been used as a means to prevent schools opting out while still retaining some control over policy for SEN.

At the other end of this continuum were clusters of a more organic nature in which schools from a defined catchment or locality collaborated over a common focus, pooling often quite small amounts of resource from their own budget for a specific purpose such as INSET, special materials or equipment or an extra teacher. Our research took place at a time of increasing local management and local responsibility and therefore increasing school budgets and possibilities for sharing parts of these. Schools were therefore being potentially torn between the conflicting pulls of collaboration and competition within a context of overall budget constraints.

Nature of SEN provision

Clusters varied in the nature of SEN provision with which they were concerned or for which they had responsibility. In theory at least the cluster could take responsibility for either non-Statemented SEN, Statemented SEN or both.

At the time of the study, the majority of LEAs retained resources for Statementing centrally and resources delegated to the cluster were therefore concerned with non-Statemented special needs. LEAs using the cluster as a level for delegating such additional resources were using this partly as a means of indicating the finite nature of the additional resources and of reducing the demand for Statements by making headteachers responsible for sharing resources and prioritising needs. This might also be interpreted as a standard decentralisation policy in the face of insufficient funding for the larger group of pupils with non-Statemented special educational needs. Thus the LEA would be delegating both the resources and the decision-making to schools. This could be perceived to have the benefits of the delegation of decision-making to the schools of a local community and of economies of scale, in that a group of schools could use the cluster resources to share a support teacher.

During the study we did not come across instances where Statemented resources had been delegated to the cluster. The closest to this could be said to be Southborough, where individual schools were additionally resourced in order to take pupils with Statements from within the cluster; however, this operated effectively as a form of special unit provision and did not involve the schools in collaboration over the provision.

It is too early to predict the effects of the 1993 legislation. The sharing of responsibility and transition between LEAs and the Funding Agency for Schools could mean that clusters become a more useful grouping for the provision of special educational needs support. The advantages would be increased responsibility and ownership amongst the schools, the possibility of a more genuine continuum of provision (non-Statemented to Statemented) and the benefits of economies of scale.

Conclusions

This chapter has aimed to present some aspects of the large number of very different cluster arrangements which are in existence across the country. Although each arrangement is complex and unique, it is possible to consider descriptive dimensions along which clusters differ, such as: origin, phase and type of schools involved, extent of collaboration, focus of collaboration, source of funding, nature of SEN provision. In the next chapter we will be looking at the ways in which different clusters operate and how their functioning affects outcomes.

CHAPTER 4

Clusters: Four Case Studies

Introduction

In the previous chapter we described some of the characteristics of
the four cluster arrangements from the case studies and, in less detail,
from the regional groups meetings. The data revealed the wide range
and diversity of arrangements of groupings of schools in the LEAs
studied. This chapter aims to consider in more detail the origins,
the operation and the outcomes of the cluster arrangements studied
and to look at some of the lessons that can be learned from these
examples. As described in Chapter 3, the research investigated the history and context of the LEA and the schools involved in the cluster,
the processes through which the cluster was set up, the way in which
the cluster operated and the outcomes for all those involved: LEA,
cluster, school, teachers and the pupils themselves. In this chapter we
attempt to explore in some depth the processes involved in setting up
and running clusters in order to elucidate some factors which appear
to be important to their functioning. We amplify the account with
quotations from the interviews.

The origins of the clusters

In the previous chapter, we described some of the ways in which the
four clusters differed in their origins and purposes. Here we will look
in greater detail at some of the processes involved in setting up the
clusters with a view to drawing some tentative conclusions about
initiating clusters.

As described in Chapter 3, the characteristics of the four clusters
were as follows:

1. Seaton cluster, Northshire LEA was a cluster of six secondary schools concentrating on provision for behaviour problems.
2. Merestoke cluster, Midshire LEA was a cluster of four primary and one secondary school. It was focused on behaviour.
3. Heathside cluster, Southborough LEA was a cluster of eight primary and one secondary school. Its focus was transition and the allocation of resources for SEN.
4. Oakridge cluster, Eastshire LEA was a cluster of 25 primary schools. Its focus was the deployment of support services and the allocation of SEN resources.

The Seaton cluster was a 'bottom up' development, in that it was not originated by the LEA, but by the local heads working in conjunction with the local senior educational psychologist (EP). The initial impetus for the collaboration came from the senior EP who had been given an extra 0.5 post for her local team. She decided to use this post to develop work within the local secondary schools. At the time, there was a lot of concern in the schools about disruptive and disaffected pupils. Corporal punishment, which had been heavily relied upon in many of the schools, had recently been abolished and schools were looking for alternative strategies for dealing with difficult pupils. In a sense, then, there was a certain opportunism at work, rather than a rationally planned development of a cluster:

> I had a half-time post, which, if I didn't involve in some kind of project work, then we would lose the use of. And the behaviour field was one which I thought the secondary schools would have no difficulty in actually working with me over.
>
> (Senior EP)

Nevertheless, there were background factors in Seaton which made it easier to establish collaboration between the schools and the EP. The town had functioned as an LEA before local government reorganisation in 1972 and had retained a strong sense of identity and feeling of local ownership of initiatives.

> But whatever we set up on a pilot basis it has always got a better chance of survival in Seaton because it is such a compact area in comparison to elsewhere. It's an area which owns its own problems in comparison to elsewhere. It's almost patriotic.
>
> (LEA officer)

The heads of the six secondary schools in Seaton had established a good relationship with each other over a long period of time. At the time when the scheme for collaboration over setting up a project concerned with behaviour was proposed, the heads (all male) had been meeting socially, once a month, over a number of years, to discuss matters of mutual interest. They had just successfully negotiated the change from 11–18 to 11–16 schools and the setting up of a sixth-form centre. There was, therefore, a history of co-operation and trust between the heads of the schools in the town.

> We have had and have a very strong bond between the comprehensive schools in Seaton that has existed for many years and still does today as far as I know, and the heads met regularly and discussed their problems so the seed bed was there for this sort of idea to germinate – what could we do within our own resources?
>
> (Former head)

Several factors which appear to be crucial to the setting up of collaborative schemes appear to have been present in Seaton:

- *A catalyst* – in the form of the senior EP who floated the idea of forming a behaviour support service from a team of teachers seconded part-time from the secondary schools.
- *Extra resources* – in the form, initially, of a 0.5 EP post to co-ordinate and train the team of teachers. Later a full-time team leader was appointed.
- *A task or problem to be solved* – in terms of the perceived difficulties schools were experiencing in dealing effectively with disruptive pupils.
- *A level of trust among the participants* – who had worked together on other problems over the years and who were peers, with equal power of veto over the collaboration.
- *A reward* – in that, initially, the collaboration was expected to provide an off-site unit for disruptive pupils. Later, the reward became the increased effectiveness of the teachers in developing in-school support for disruptive pupils.
- *A co-ordinator* – initially the senior EP, later the team leader, who was answerable to the heads of the schools for the performance of the team.

These factors were also present in some form in the Merestoke cluster in Midshire LEA. The crucial difference between Merestoke and Seaton was that Midshire was interested in and actively promoted collaboration between its schools. Schools in Midshire had been grouped in single-phase clusters for work on the National Curriculum. They had also been grouped into cross-phase partnerships. The clusters were groups of primary schools which came together for curriculum development work, in the main. The partnerships were groupings of a secondary school and around nine primary schools, within a certain catchment area. The cluster we studied in Midshire was, in fact, a partnership in their terminology. The development of the partnerships had been patchy: some were much more active than others, and the LEA was keen to promote the idea of working within partnerships.

The money provided by the GEST (Grants for Education Support and Training) funding had thus provided the opportunity to achieve two objectives:

> To look at behaviour from a point of view that looked at systems rather than how to deal on a day-to-day basis with individual pupils. . . . To give more of a push to partnership-type working . . . so there was a kind of twin thrust there.
>
> (LEA officer)

Although the initiation of the collaboration had come from the LEA, and LEA officers and advisers played a significant role in setting the parameters for the project we studied, the day-to-day running of the activity and the management of it was left to the schools themselves.

> Well, the fundamental aim was to look at pupils' behaviour and schools were free to define their own terms.
>
> (LEA adviser)

This reflected the LEA's policy of allowing autonomy to schools, within an overall policy framework.

The *catalyst* for the collaboration was the LEA officer who was charged with using GEST money for staff development in the area of behaviour and discipline in schools. He, along with colleagues, devised a scheme which required schools to put in joint bids for the use of the money. Again, as in the Seaton initiative, there was an element of opportunism at work, in that the GEST bid had been successful, and in discussing how the funding should be used, it was decided to address the issue of behaviour by promoting partnership activities.

Well, we were allocated this money and decided that this was the way
of spending it.

(EP)

We looked at ways of spending the money and came up with the
model that's been implemented.

(LEA adviser)

The *extra resources* consisted of a sum of money (around £2,000 per
group of schools) which could be used to provide supply cover to
release teachers to work on joint planning and other joint activities
(such as inter-school visits). Not all the schools used all the money,
and some was subsequently allocated to hold a conference at which
feedback was given about the progress of the various projects undertaken by the partnerships.

The *task* set by the LEA was to devise an inter-school programme
which would promote collaboration and which would address the issue
of behaviour in schools. The groups of schools were also required to
account for their use of the funds and to describe their joint work at a conference held one year after the start of the projects. This strand of accountability was important in focusing the groups towards some observable
achievement within the first year of the project.

There was already a level of *trust* between the schools, since they had
worked as a partnership on other joint activities. The secondary school
was held in high regard by the primary schools and they were interested
in developing their links with the secondary school. It is interesting to
note that in another partnership group within the LEA, a secondary
school had approached a number of nearby primary schools to put
forward a joint bid, and had been rebuffed because the primary schools
did not want to associate themselves with the secondary school which
had recently been the subject of some bad publicity about bullying.

The *reward* for participating schools was a chance to improve links
(which was seen as important by the primaries and the secondary
school) and also the opportunity to work on a problem which, whilst
not acute in many of the schools, nevertheless was seen as in need of
some development both in policy and in practice.

The *co-ordinator* of the group was a senior teacher in the secondary
school who had been responsible for drawing the schools together to
make the initial bid for funding and had subsequently convened and
chaired meetings and had provided much of the drive to keep the collaboration going.

The Midshire example is interesting because it demonstrates how an LEA can set the parameters and provide the stimulus for collaboration between schools. However, even in an LEA which promotes collaboration, there are still a number of school groupings which do not actively work together. For the first round of bids for funding, the LEA received five bids out of 30 possible. In the second round, twelve bids were received, as schools which had successful projects acted as exemplars for schools which were less advanced in collaboration. This indicates that the level of mutual trust and perceived advantage to be gained from collaboration takes some time to develop.

The clusters in Southborough and in Eastshire had been set up, originally, for administrative purposes. In Southborough, the links between first, middle and secondary schools were the focus of the clusters, and this structure enabled provision for special educational needs to be developed on a cluster basis. The focus of the links was *transition* rather than collaboration to enhance SEN provision. A report by the director of education calls for a child with special needs 'to be able to progress from first to middle to high school'.

In Southborough, the purpose of the LEA development of additionally resourced mainstream schools (ARMS) within some clusters was to enable pupils with SEN to be educated within their local community, thus furthering the authority's policy of integration. 'As stepping stones towards integration across the Borough, it would be helpful to identify clusters of schools which would share responsibility for children with special educational needs' (Director's Report).

It is interesting to note that, although the ARMS provided a resource for the cluster group of schools, it did not involve the schools themselves in collaboration or 'sharing responsibility'; rather, pupils with particular SEN were moved from one mainstream school within a cluster which was not additionally resourced, to another which was and where their needs could be met from the additional resourcing. The motivation of the schools was a significant factor in Southborough, since schools were asked to bid to become ARMS schools, and tended to be schools which had already had some experience in providing for pupils with SEN.

The Eastshire clusters also had the aim of enhancing provision for SEN within local areas. The LEA's policy was one of devolving resources to local areas and the enhancement of local provision to provide a 'one-stop shop' for SEN. The focus in Eastshire was upon clusters of primary schools. The administration of the statutory assessment procedures and of provision of support for non-Statemented children was organised on a cluster basis. The links were not so much between the schools as between the support staff (psychologists, doctors, support teachers, speech therapists, etc) who served the schools.

Both in Southborough and in Eastshire there was a potential for collaboration between the schools, which was, at the time of our study, as yet undeveloped. Some key elements were missing, such as a *task focus* and the availability of *extra resources* to promote collaborative activities. The same level of *trust* between the partners was not evident, nor was there a *reward* for collaboration in terms of enhanced provision. Schools in the Oakridge cluster in Eastshire saw the LEA as the provider of resources for SEN, and in the Southborough clusters, the extra resources were located in one or two schools and not perceived as cluster resources.

The operation of the clusters

The four clusters had, as described in Chapter 3 and above, different origins, aims and structures. They also had different approaches to organising their work. The Seaton cluster was managed by the heads of the six schools involved. They decided at the beginning of each school year how much teacher time they would second to the behaviour support team and they met regularly with the full-time team leader throughout the year to review the operation of the scheme.

A crucial role was played by the team leader in liaising with the heads, informing them of the work of the team and discussing any problems with them. The role of the team leader had changed over the time that the cluster had operated, in that its success had led the LEA to reorganise the county behaviour support service and to create support teams in other areas of the county. The Seaton scheme was then incorporated into the overall County scheme, but with the difference that, in Seaton, the heads continued to contribute their teachers to the team, and therefore still exercised a great deal of control over the service: 'We all have a vested interest as our staff are still working on the project, so we still have a management role in there' (headteacher).

The team leader, then, had two lines of management – to the heads and to the head of the County support service. This indicates that it is possible for clusters to involve joint management, by headteachers, of resources delegated by the LEA. The role of the leader as a co-ordinator and interface between the team of teachers and the heads was seen as crucial to the success of the scheme, but the commitment of the heads to the scheme was also crucial:

> I think the positive factors as I would see them were a commitment from headteachers. Getting senior management to back something is vital. And the fact that they put the teacher time in, which is a very valuable commodity and their constant watching of what went on were very important setting up features.
>
> (Team leader)

Another vital ingredient which contributed to the successful operation and continuance of the scheme was the fact that it was perceived as effective by the schools:

> It wasn't just because the heads were so able, though they clearly managed the thing; it wasn't just because the team leader was a very able teacher; it wasn't just because the psychological services were behind it and the LEA put resources into it. It was because, whatever the chemistry was, it helped the basic classroom teacher, and I mean that's really why it's been so successful.
>
> (LEA officer)

These supportive factors were also present in the Merestoke cluster. The cluster co-ordinator was a highly respected senior teacher from the secondary school who was adept at promoting the joint activities required.

> It's chaired very well. B--- always has a clear agenda, and he moves it forward all the time. We have set tasks to do and he's very good at asking people to report back and he's a good timekeeper so we know we're going to get through a set amount of work.
>
> (Primary head)

This indicates that busy people like heads will not begrudge the time involved in collaboration if they can see it is well managed and task orientated. However, the co-ordinator himself was aware that he was driving the scheme and wondered whether the team was too accepting of his suggestions:

> Sometimes I would worry that we've got people who would just put

their hands up and say 'OK let's do that.' You know, that we've got people being led as opposed to people coming together and saying, you know, a little bit more ... um ... if you like, positive conflict.

(Cluster co-ordinator)

So there may be dangers to the continuity of a scheme if it relies too heavily on the drive and commitment of one person.

However, the cluster in Merestoke had another source of support. As part of the LEA's commitment to fostering successful collaborative working between schools, each project within the Midshire scheme had been allocated a 'mentor' or 'facilitator' from the central team, which was administering the GEST funding. The Merestoke cluster had been allocated an experienced adviser who had been useful to the cluster team in helping them to identify their goals and priorities and supporting their collaborative work. Her role had been 'to draw the group together and make our development more purposeful' (primary head). She brought an 'outside perspective' to the group's work. The facilitator commented:

And what's said to me is that you have to support people. You can't just expect partnership projects to happen.

(Adviser)

If you look at the results, the ones where there had been better work going on, were the ones where there had been a better quality of support. And that does not necessarily mean time. It's something to do with experience and with chemistry.

(Adviser)

This help from the centre, as well as being facilitative, also sent the message that the collaborative project was seen as important by senior figures within the LEA.

Another key figure in the Merestoke cluster was the local SEN advisory and support teacher. She had not originally been involved in the project, but had contacted the co-ordinator and asked to be involved. Her expertise and her knowledge of the primary schools within the cluster had made her a significant contributor to the work of the project.

These factors illustrate further aspects of cluster organisation which appear to be important in the maintenance of successful collaboration over time:

The role of the co-ordinator

This appears to be a key factor in the maintenance of the cluster activity. In both Merestoke and Seaton the co-ordinators were people who commanded the respect and trust both of the schools involved and of the LEA. They were senior members of staff. The co-ordinators acted as the interface between the work of the group and the management, both at school and LEA levels. They supported the cluster in planning and organising the work to be done and provided accountability for the use of resources delegated to the cluster. Since the co-ordinator has to act as the negotiator between the schools, it is vital that he or she is of sufficient seniority to carry out that task effectively.

For clusters where the initiative has come from the LEA, the help of a facilitator to support, but not to control, the work of the cluster seems to have been a positive factor.

Ownership

The heads of the schools involved in the Seaton cluster felt that they 'owned' the initiative and that they had a stake in its success. This sense of ownership and control was sustained even after the LEA became more involved. The peer-group pressure exerted by the heads on each other meant that no one person or group became dominant. The initiative was jointly owned by the schools.

> We cohere so well as a group [of heads] that any problems can be sorted out quite frankly and out in the open and we didn't fall out.
>
> (Headteacher)

In Merestoke, although the LEA had initiated the project, the day-to-day running was left to the schools and this allowed a sense of ownership to emerge. There was some sense among the schools that the project was being driven by the secondary school, but the skill of the co-ordinator and the support of the SEN advisory teacher (who was primary based) maintained a balance in which the primary schools felt that their contribution was valuable and valued.

> There was a positive feeling of (a) being included and (b) addressing an issue which does crop up sufficiently regularly, even in a small school, to be of some concern.
>
> (SEN advisory teacher)

Effectiveness

A perception that the initiative was effective in addressing the problems it had been set up to solve was also an important factor. Positive feedback from teachers was an important component in sustaining the commitment to continue to share resources. Those involved in both the Merestoke and the Seaton clusters, in different ways, perceived the collaborations to be successful.

> The amount of time we put in is more than amply repaid by what we get out of it and I think all the schools are still committed to it.
>
> (Headteacher, Seaton)

Two further aspects of cluster organisation also appear to be important to success. These are:

Size

The two actively collaborative clusters we studied were relatively small – five schools in the Merestoke cluster and six schools in Seaton. The larger groupings (nine schools in Heathside and 25 schools in Oakridge) had not developed any significant collaborative activity (although, it must be said, that this was not part of the purpose of the Eastshire scheme which had set up the Oakridge cluster. There had been an intention, in Southborough LEA to devolve control over some SEN resources to clusters, but this had never been realised). Given the difficulties of arranging meetings, agreeing on objectives and carrying out joint tasks, it may be less feasible for large clusters to undertake any significant collaborative activities. In rural areas, it is relatively simple to define cross-phase clusters, since there is usually only one secondary school available (as in Merestoke).

> It's very clear who's working with whom and there are clear benefits on all sides and people are accepting and realising that.
>
> (Adviser)

In urban areas, it may not be as easy for 'pyramid' clusters to be set up, although most secondary schools are likely to have one or two primary schools which are major suppliers of pupils to them. In such cases, it may be simpler for clusters to involve the major primary/secondary partners. An alternative is for a group of primary or a group of secondary schools to form a cluster. Seaton is an example of a successful cluster of secondary schools. The 'parity of esteem' among schools in single-phase clusters may make it easier for partnership to be sustained, as the Seaton example shows. The schools in Seaton had varying catchment areas, and some of the schools were less popular than others, but a sense that the problem of disruptive behaviour was a problem shared by all schools was one reason that a joint solution was found.

Complexity

The Merestoke and Seaton collaborations were kept relatively simple, in that they concentrated on one specific area of SEN, that is, behaviour. There had been other collaborative projects in Merestoke, but they did not run concurrently. In Seaton, the behaviour support project was not generalised to deal with wider SEN, although there had been some discussion about whether this would be feasible.

Taken together, these two factors – size and complexity – indicate that successful collaboration can be maintained if projects remain manageable in scope. If a project becomes large and complex, then the time taken up in meetings, the loss of control, and thus of a sense of ownership and the more diffuse nature of the task, might put greater strains on the collaboration. Over time, successful collaborations in one area might give schools the confidence to widen the scope of collaborative activities, but we found no example of this during our research.

There might, in fact, be some drawbacks in too extensive and too close collaboration between schools, in that it might become overly bureaucratic and might limit choices for parents. For example, schools might formulate arrangements so that, within a cluster, they might specialise in meeting particular needs. If parents were then expected to place their child in the school which had specialised resources and were prevented from using another school, this would limit their choice of school. Although parents are entitled to 'express a preference' for the school of their choice, this does not guarantee a place and, for children with Statements, the criterion of 'efficient use of resources' could be used to limit parental choice.

Some difficult aspects

As well as factors which enhanced collaboration, we also found some aspects of the process of setting up and running the clusters which had negative effects. Some of these were the obverse of the positive factors already described, for example, *lack of consultation* with the heads of the schools involved had led to some confusion about the purpose of the clusters in Eastshire. Although collaboration between the schools had not been the goal of the clusters, nevertheless, a new way of working and accessing resources had been imposed which left some heads and teachers confused. This lack of consultation and preparation by the central team had led to initial difficulties in operating the new system of referrals of children to the multi-disciplinary panel. However, the goodwill of the professionals involved had overcome these initial difficulties.

Another factor which caused problems for the collaborative activities was that, among some groups, there had been initial *confusion about the nature of the task* they had set themselves and the ways in which they were to accomplish it. For example, in the Merestoke cluster, the heads and teachers involved decided to undertake observations of pupils' behaviour in each others' schools. However, some of them thought that they were to undertake detailed and systematic observations of individuals and others thought that they were to observe more generally the ways in which other schools tackled behaviour problems. This lack of clarity led to a certain amount of frustration and disillusionment for some teachers.

The lack of a shared focus for activity led to declining interest in collaboration in the Heathside cluster in Southborough. Initially, there had been joint meetings of SEN staff in the first and middle schools across the cluster, to discuss issues of mutual interest and to share some in-service training activities. However, the meetings became less and less frequent because of 'the lack of an agreed agenda'. This indicates that, unless there is a specific on-going task to be undertaken, collaboration is unlikely to be sustained. Although improved communication and relationships between schools are desired outcomes of cluster activity, they appear to be by-products of the process of working together on specific tasks.

Lack of time to attend meetings and pressure of work were other factors which made collaboration more difficult. But, in the clusters we studied, the positives outweighed the negatives and the groups found ways to tackle problems and overcome difficulties. A key motivation in this was the sense that there were positive outcomes for pupils.

Anything to do with children at heart will motivate teachers to participate.

(Primary head)

Outcomes of clusters

For pupils

It was difficult to measure the outcome of the collaboration in terms of its effects on individual pupils. This was in part due to the timescale and scope of the research project, in part because the source of outcomes (for SEN) is difficult to isolate and to attribute. However, in general terms, positive outcomes for pupils were noted in the clusters. In Seaton, the numbers of pupils excluded from school or recommended for a Statement for behaviour problems had dropped significantly since the setting up of the project. Individual children interviewed by the project team had been aware that help from the behaviour support teachers had enabled them to overcome some of their problems in school.

In the Heathside cluster, children with Statements had been enabled to remain within their local area, rather than be sent to a special school. In Oakridge, pupils had benefited from the allocation of extra resources to support them and from the closer liaison between professionals from different services, which enabled a co-ordinated approach to their problems to be taken.

Some respondents felt that children had benefited in less tangible ways:

> The fact that colleagues come from other schools and bring lots of fresh ideas ... and they become almost like a neutral ear to the children ... that's what I would say the real success was. It was something we hadn't had before, and that they were people from another school.
>
> (Headteacher, Seaton)

For teachers and other professionals

One of the most consistently positive outcomes for teachers and other professionals in all the clusters studied was a sense of improved communication between staff. This was highly valued, as was the breakdown of isolation which some teachers had experienced in trying to deal with pupils with SEN. Improved communication had resulted in teachers realising that the problems which they were trying to solve in relation to children with special educational needs were not peculiar to them or to their school, but were widespread. It also acted as a moderating influence, which led some teachers to realise that problems which they had thought were severe, were, in fact, relatively mild.

I've made relationships with staff that I knew tentatively. I've renewed relationships with children who were very pleased to see me. I've had the opportunity to become perhaps more aware of the similarities and differences between teaching styles and teaching approaches and staff—pupil relationships in both sectors.

(SEN advisory teacher)

For many of the teachers, participation in collaborative projects had been a powerful source of development — both of their sense of capability and of their knowledge and skills in dealing with special educational needs. The Seaton project had an explicit staff development aspect, but, even in those projects which did not have this element, staff felt that they had benefited in this way.

I feel an immeasurably better teacher through seeing other schools.

(Class teacher)

I think it's the most exciting thing I've been involved in, during my time in education. I think it's certainly jogged a lot of people out of ruts.... The spin-off was you got on other courses and other new things that were happening.

(Support teacher)

Clusters had made the links between schools and the routes to gaining access to support more open and explicit, and staff reported that they were now clearer about how to access extra help for pupils — even though the extra help was not always forthcoming.

I'm aware of all the mechanisms that exist and I feel I shouldn't act alone in these things. Many years ago, teaching, I would have felt that my classes were self-contained.

(Class teacher)

For the schools involved

The clusters had given the schools access to resources which they might not otherwise have had. They were able to share expertise, to learn from each other and generally to develop policies and, in some cases, provision which would support children with special educational needs.

Those groups of schools that did manage to keep on working and meeting together and producing things, those were seen by people themselves as positive and hopefully they've developed sufficient strengths from that to be able to continue.

(Adviser, Midshire)

The heads of the schools reported increased confidence and competence in the staff who had been involved. The schools in the Seaton cluster also reported reductions in problems of discipline.

Schools have become more efficient and self-sufficient in dealing with problems because of the support.

(Year head, Seaton)

I think all the schools are learning to cope with their problems themselves.

(Support teacher, Seaton)

For the LEA

The cluster groupings gave the LEA a more systematic way of dealing with schools and allocating resources. This was the major administrative benefit of the clusters.

In Northshire, the Seaton cluster scheme had become a model for the deployment of support staff for behaviour problems throughout the county. The Seaton scheme had resulted in a significant drop in referrals for statutory assessment of pupils with behaviour problems from that area, which had demonstrated the potential of the scheme to reduce the rate in other areas of the county.

In Midshire, the scheme had further enhanced the county's policy of creating partnerships between schools, which was particularly beneficial for small rural primary schools. This appeared to be a cost-effective way of enhancing the resources and support available to small rural schools. It also provided a smooth transition from primary to secondary school.

In Southborough, the aim of the scheme had been to improve transition, and it appeared that the majority of pupils from primary schools transferred to a secondary school within their cluster. Resourcing some schools within a cluster for pupils with Statements had enabled the borough's policy of integration to be progressed.

The Eastshire clusters had enabled the LEA to rationalise its system for the administration of special needs provision. It had brought staff from education, health and social services together on a regular basis, and had provided the basis for a moderation of demands for support from schools within the cluster.

At all levels, inter-school collaboration was reported to have increased workloads for staff. However, the benefits of collaboration had outweighed the costs, and in all clusters studied, the balance of outcomes appears to have been positive, which was a powerful reinforcing factor in the maintenance of the collaborative activities.

Conclusion

This chapter has raised some general points about the processes involved in setting up and running clusters, based on the detailed study of clusters in four LEAs. Although the four clusters were different in their origins, structures and objectives, there have been some common issues arising from a study of the processes involved. These issues give some indications of the factors to be borne in mind by those, in LEAs and schools, who might wish to move towards setting up clusters in their own localities. The final chapter of this book offers some suggestions about how headteachers, governors or LEA staff might approach the task of setting up and operating some form of collaborative arrangement for provision for pupils with special educational needs.

CHAPTER 5

Developing Clusters

Introduction

As we discussed in Chapter 1, schools face difficult choices about how to carry out their responsibilities for pupils with special educational needs. With the new Code of Practice, which spells out what is expected from schools, headteachers and governors, they will be looking for ways to enhance and develop their capabilities to provide for special educational needs. In this chapter we suggest ways in which those involved in providing for pupils with SEN can plan and develop arrangements for inter-school collaboration. We discuss who might be interested in developing clusters and what interests they may have in so doing. Drawing on findings from our research study we then outline some of the key considerations which would need to be taken into account in setting up a cluster arrangement. Any such development in the current climate of schooling also needs to consider how to go about school development planning. We, therefore, look at the development of clusters in terms of some relevant and useful models and approaches to the management of change. Without wanting to go into unnecessary detail about what such development strategies would consist of, we then suggest some possible activities which might support the development of cluster arrangements. We include some workshop materials for these activities derived from the outcomes of our research conducted into clusters for SEN.

It is important in setting out approaches to developing clusters that we are clear what is meant by a cluster. As we found in the research which informs this book, there have been different versions of clusters, some of which do not involve inter-school collaboration. Without going into a detailed explanation, our working definition is worth restating here:

A cluster is a grouping of schools with a relatively stable and long-term commitment to share some resources and decision-making about an area of school activity. The arrangements are likely to involve a degree of formality such as regular meetings to plan and monitor this activity, and some loss of autonomy through the need for negotiated decision-making.

In outlining ways of developing clusters, it is useful to keep in mind what is being developed and, by implication, what is not being developed. From the definition it will be clear that what is being developed is a system which involves joint decision-making about the use of shared resources in an arrangement which has some stability and formality. What is not being developed is a short-term arrangement in which schools have a few exchanges of teachers or children. This chapter is not about setting up links between individual schools. It is about the more extensive and formal types of arrangements we have described in the previous chapters.

Who would be interested in developing clusters and why?

From the descriptions of the various forms of cluster arrangement described in Chapter 3, it will be clear that clusters can arise from initiatives taken by schools and by LEAs in conjunction with schools. Those who might be interested in the actual planning and setting up of clusters will be people who have responsibilities for SEN provision in schools and LEAs:

- headteachers and governors of schools;
- SEN teachers and co-ordinators in schools;
- LEA officers and inspectors;
- educational psychologists and others in LEA support services.

We should also take into account the perspective of managers of health and social services who provide for children with difficulties in the community. Their position will be discussed briefly. There is also a parental perspective on inter-school collaboration for SEN and it is important to recognise this. But whether this implies that parents would be interested in the detailed planning of a cluster is another matter. Those involved in initiating a cluster arrangement need to address this question. It may be that parents of pupils with SEN in a school envisaging a cluster would be more interested in participating than other parents. Those wishing to set up a cluster may find it useful to consult parents or parents' representatives about the idea and to take their views into account when making their plans.

In discussing how the various stakeholders might see clusters as a useful way for maintaining and enhancing provision for SEN, it is worth making explicit the assumption behind this analysis. In trying to understand how key people might come to gain a commitment to a proposed change, we must attempt to understand how these groups might judge how the change might affect them both positively and negatively – what benefits and what costs the change might have for them. These issues have already been discussed in some detail in Chapter 2.

Such a cost-benefit approach deals with general factors which are related to each other in fairly loose ways, but which give a useful view about how commitment to change might arise. One factor is the degree to which people feel dissatisfaction with the way things have been and are currently organised. As regards arrangements for SEN provision, this is about how dissatisfied the groups mentioned above are with the current organisation and quality of provision. Another key factor is the extent to which those involved have a clear and positive view of the outcomes of the change. This involves not only working out a clear vision of the benefits of the future arrangements, but ensuring that there is something of benefit for nearly everybody. A third factor which is important for gaining commitment to change is that those involved see what practical first steps would get the change going. It is one thing to feel the need for change and to have some general idea of the benefits of where you are heading towards, but quite another to see what immediate steps will get you going. Without seeing these first practical steps the force for change can be inhibited. It is then important to consider how these three general factors are weighed against the costs of the change in financial, organisational and psychological terms. With a view to developing clusters, this involves trying to identify the benefits and the obstacles and difficulties which need to be faced in the setting up process.

It is within a framework of thinking along these lines that we will now consider how the four key groups of people might regard the planning of SEN clusters.

Headteachers and governors of schools

Headteachers and governors are likely to regard the prospect of setting up clusters for SEN in the context of the growth of their responsibilities arising from the operation of Local Management of Schools and the general moves to more systematic approaches to school development planning. As provision for SEN is an important part of the management and development of an ordinary school, heads and governors could see inter-school collaboration as offering a promising practical approach. This is especially relevant with the extension of SEN requirements placed on schools following the 1993 Education Act and the recent Code of SEN Practice. As explained in Chapter 1, this will require schools to develop and report on their SEN policy and practices.

Even without these new responsibilities, heads and governors would have been aware and many have become concerned about the gaps left by reductions in LEA support services. We have referred in previous chapters to the increasing requests by schools for statutory assessment and Statements as a way of ensuring security of support for children with SEN. Some heads would also have been aware of the resources they receive for pupils with SEN under LMS. However, many other headteachers may not be aware of the amounts in their budgets which relate to SEN. The Audit Commission found that more than half the headteachers in their sample were not sufficiently clear about these amounts (Audit Commission/HMI 1992). More than half the heads also thought that their schools were not given the level of funding they believed that they needed for pupils with SEN.

Heads and governors of LEA and grant-maintained schools alike need to be clearer about these SEN budgetary matters which bear directly on schools' own assessments of what resources are available for enhancing provision for SEN. Heads and governors would also need more specific definitions of what responsibilities their schools have for pupils with SEN who do not have a Statement. This matter has been dealt with in the recent Code of Practice and the 1993 Education Act.

As well as the duties given to governing bodies under the 1981 Act, there is a requirement to have a policy for SEN and to report on this policy annually to the parents.

The policy must include:

1. Basic information about the school's special educational provision:
    ● the name of the school's SEN co-ordinator;
    ● admissions arrangements;

- any SEN specialism and any special units;
- any building adaptations and special facilities.

2. Information about the school's policies for identification, assessment and provision for all pupils with SEN:
   - the school's objectives for pupils with SEN;
   - identification, assessment, monitoring and review procedures;
   - use of any staged approach to identifying and meeting special educational needs;
   - policy on access to the National Curriculum;
   - policy and priorities for the allocation of resources to pupils with SEN;
   - integration arrangements within the school;
   - criteria for monitoring the success of the school's SEN policy.

3. Information about the school's staffing policies and partnerships with bodies beyond the school:
   - staff experience and qualifications;
   - the school's SEN in-service training policy;
   - arrangements for partnership with parents;
   - use made of external support services;
   - links with special schools and other resource centres;
   - links with medical and social services and any voluntary organisations.

There are obviously significant resource implications attached to implementing these guidelines on school SEN policy. Even though schools have funding for SEN included within their budgets, many headteachers and governors are concerned that this funding is already under pressure because of the other demands on schools' resources. This is where the pooling of funds with other schools has considerable benefits in enabling schools to share in economies of scale. For example, in order to employ a qualified specialist SEN teacher or extra classroom assistants, pooled funds are more likely to put schools in a position to employ full-time teachers and assistants of high quality and to purchase expensive materials and equipment, if these are needed. Cluster arrangements may also enable schools to provide joint in-service training, or to make better use of specialist facilities which already exist within the cluster but which may be under-utilised by one school, for example equipment for visually or hearing impaired pupils.

Heads and governors will also be aware that successful inter-school collaboration over some specific activity can have other wider and perhaps unforeseen positive consequences. Experience of school management and development shows that positive developments in one area can become the basis for further positive developments in other areas. A development such as clustering for SEN can be seen from this perspective to offer a whole which is more than the sum of the parts. For heads and governors who have become concerned about the increasingly competitive environment in which their schools operate, SEN and other forms of inter-school collaboration also offer a viable way of expressing their solidarity with other schools. In this sense, inter-school collaboration has a wider value in the current context.

SEN teachers and co-ordinators in schools

Many of the concerns of headteachers and governors which could lead them to be interested in clusters are also felt by SEN teachers and co-ordinators in schools. The position of SEN teachers and co-ordinators, however, might be that they find that their headteachers and governors do not fully appreciate the problems of providing adequately for SEN pupils. Being in daily contact with pupils with SEN and class teachers, SEN teachers and co-ordinators are the group most likely to be aware of gaps in SEN provision in their schools. These gaps will be made more apparent by the demands placed on schools by the Code of Practice outlined above. This could put them in a position where they need to find ways to bring these gaps to the attention of headteachers and governors. How they might do this will be covered in the following sections of this chapter.

SEN teachers and co-ordinators also have their own concerns which might lead them to be interested in setting up some kind of cluster arrangement. As described in Chapter 3, advisers and inspectors in some LEAs have set up regular meetings of SEN teachers and co-ordinators to keep them in contact with each other and to enable them to learn from each other. These contacts are important for teachers, especially lone teachers with full-time SEN responsibilities. With the declining role of LEAs in setting up cross-school links, SEN teachers and co-ordinators might come to feel more isolated from their colleagues in other schools. Cluster arrangements would enable SEN teachers to reforge such contacts and derive the wider benefits of collaboration.

LEA officers and inspectors

Despite the changing role of LEA officers and inspectors since the implementation of the 1988 and subsequent Education Acts, their concerns remain basically similar to those who are in daily contact with pupils or from those who manage schools. However, their concerns are more broadly based because their position gives them a wider view of the need to provide support services for all schools in the LEA. As our research has shown, some LEA officers and inspectors have experienced difficulties in organising services because of the loss of economies of scale following the delegation of funds to individual schools. The Audit Commission report also showed that some LEAs have expressed reservations about delegating funds for pupils with SEN (Audit Commission/HMI 1992). They identified problems around two areas, firstly, worries that delegated funds might not be spent on the pupils with SEN, and secondly, the belief that LEA teams had more expertise than teachers in ordinary schools in providing for pupils with some types of SEN.

The Code of Practice envisages a continuing role for LEA support teams, as providers of advice and support at stage 3 level of intervention and beyond. With problems such as limited resources and increasing demands for services to resolve, LEA officers and inspectors could look to cluster arrangements as a useful way forward, and as our research has shown, some have done so. LEAs could assist schools which pool some of their SEN-related funds in setting up cluster arrangements. They could do this in different ways:

1. by being supportive of schools which take cluster initiatives;
2. by offering to top-up funds to schools willing to use their own devolved funds for clustering; or
3. by offering to devolve funds to groups of schools on condition that they set up a cluster.

Each of these solutions has been tried by one or more of the LEAs which participated in this research.

In these ways, LEAs can maintain the benefits deriving from economies of scale and, at the same time, have more confidence that the funds were being used to support pupils with SEN in appropriate ways. So cluster arrangements would give LEA officers and inspectors a way forward which meets their some of their concerns about the loss of control through delegation, whilst offering them a facilitating role in developing new systems of SEN support in ordinary schools.

Educational psychologists and others in LEA support services

With some part of the funding of Educational Psychology Services (EPS) being retained by LEAs, at least for the advice needed for Statutory Assessment, there is an assured future for educational psychologists (EPs) in the future pattern of services for pupils with SEN. However, EPs have had a broader and a more balanced conception of their work and contribution which included advice and preventive work for schools as being indispensable to their statutory assessment advice to LEAs. To maintain this balance of work EPS will increasingly have to relate to schools, which now control their own funds and can act as the purchasers of their own support services. This would mean that EPs would need to negotiate service contracts with schools.

In this changing context, EPS might find that a cluster arrangement would be useful to them as the unit with which they can negotiate their service contracts. A group of schools would be better able to estimate their needs for EPS collectively than on an individual school-by-school basis. Schools might also be better able to articulate their common and individual needs to educational psychologists when doing so collectively. From their side, educational psychologists might be able to provide services to the cluster of schools which they could not do so effectively when working individually with schools, for example, in-service training and organisational development consultancy work.

Support teachers are in a more vulnerable position than EPs, since their continued existence is not assured. Many LEAs are cutting back on support teaching teams or changing their method of funding so that they are working on an agency basis. If LEAs decide to delegate resources for support teaching to schools, it might be in the interests of support teams to explore with schools the possibility of groups of schools pooling their resources to fund a number of teachers to serve clusters of schools. As described in Chapter 3, some LEAs have already devolved funds for support teachers to clusters of schools and left it to the schools to decide how best to use those resources.

Delegation to clusters would have the advantage of retaining expertise within a team and of providing schools with a stable team of teachers to support SEN. The provision for less common special needs, such as sensory impairment, might serve a number of clusters within an LEA.

Managers of social and health services

The general promotion of a multi-professional and multi-service approach to children was strongly advocated by the Warnock Report and is widely acknowledged to be a very beneficial for children with special needs (Davie 1993). It is also stressed as an important issue by the Code of Practice. One of the perceived advantages of clusters, as proposed by the Fish Report, was that they could be a focus for multi-service work. So, managers of social and health services are another group which might have an interest in the development of clusters for SEN. Our research, however, did not show many examples of this multi-professional aspect of clusters. Where there was such an aspect (in the Eastshire case study) this was when the grouping of schools was organised by the LEA and there was little direct inter-school collaboration.

It could be that when schools collaborate to share a teaching resource that it is not obvious that it would be useful to co-ordinate and link this with medical and social work contributions. This does not imply that social and health services have no role in developing clusters, but that the initiative might better lie with those in schools and LEAs to initiate these links. This could be done by bringing social and health service representatives into cluster planning activities. Such an approach has been used in some previous work done by some of the authors when supporting LEAs in their review and development of their statutory assessment procedures (Evans *et al.* 1989).

What development approaches are available for establishing clusters?

When the groups outlined above have an interest in developing clusters, they need to find some way to translate their interests into practical and co-ordinated plans. This is when an understanding of the management and development of schools and skills in planning developments are so important. Readers are likely to be familiar with some of the general frameworks for school review and development, such as, the Guidelines for Review and Internal Development in Schools, GRIDS (Abbott *et al.* 1988) and school development planning (Hargreaves and Hopkins 1991). What these and other similar approaches have to offer are systematic stage-by-stage ways of undertaking a development process. These systematic approaches express various basic principles which include:

- data-based assessment and analysis of where the school is;
- identifying priorities by a process which takes account of a wide range of views and values;

- designing plans in terms of outcomes and routes to them, taking account of resource considerations;
- formulating action plans which are specific about success criteria, timing and responsibilities;
- consulting with interested parties and seeking endorsement for plans;
- reviewing progress towards planned goals as part of an on-going cyclical process.

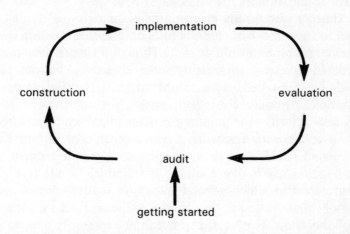

Figure 5.1 The school development planning cycle

For example, Hargreaves and Hopkins outline a simple development cycle, as shown in Figure 5.1. In their framework, auditing includes reviewing the organisation's strengths and weaknesses; construction involves setting priorities for development and then turning them into specific targets; implementation involves putting into action the planned priorities and targets; and evaluation is about checking the success of the development.

A framework for general school development planning like the one above is the most appropriate context in which to consider the specific development of a SEN cluster. However, those who wish to start from *general* school reviews need to be aware of the possibility that the process of whole-school development planning could relegate the development of a SEN cluster to a marginal activity. This can happen if a school does not have an established and successful practice of development planning and when other pressing needs arise in the audit or review stage of the process. One can expect to find these conditions in the current context of rapid and major change in the school system.

Working within the context of a school's development planning there could be two starting points which might lead to the setting up of a SEN cluster. The first is when the development priority is about special educational needs. The second is when the development priority is about enhancing the school's external relations. With either starting point, there can be no assurance that, when priorities are translated into development targets, a cluster approach will emerge as the best arrangement to meet the school's SEN priority.

When starting with a SEN priority, the planning process might lead the school to focus more on internal SEN developments within the limited financial resources available to it. Though a cluster scheme might be considered as a way of meeting some objectives, various factors which will be discussed below, might weigh a decision against the cluster option. Alternatively, when starting with a school's external relations as a priority, the planning process might lead the school to focus on a collaboration scheme in some other area of activity not directly related to SEN, such as transition of pupils from primary school or joint INSET. We found, for example, in our research, a transition cluster in which general transition matters dominated the inter-school collaboration at the expense of the particular SEN aspects of the collaboration. However, this need not necessarily happen if the SEN aspects are carefully planned and protected. Ideally the planned linking of SEN inter-school collaboration with collaboration over other activities, such as transition, can strengthen the SEN aspects.

These comments about how SEN cluster arrangements may or may not emerge from general whole-school development planning are important reminders to those interested in the cluster approach to be aware of some of potential pitfalls in development planning from a SEN perspective. However, cluster arrangements are significant and effective organisational means by which schools can enhance their provision for SEN. Awareness of their potential and limitations in the context of development planning can enable schools to pursue targets or objectives, which they might otherwise set aside for want of available means to realise. Knowledge about cluster arrangements is therefore in itself an important part of development planning. It is important, then, that those with an interest in developing provision for SEN in schools, ensure that the potential of clusters for enhancing a school's ability to make provision, is demonstrated to those involved in the development-planning cycle.

Although all significant school developments might be expected to arise from development planning according to principles about school management and development, some changes might arise from initiatives which do not form part of the systematic cycle of internal review and development. These could be initiatives which arise from outside the school, such as those stemming from the LEA, which might themselves arise from some government directives, such as the new Code of Practice for SEN. In this context, those involved in responding to initiatives of this kind may find it helpful to adopt a systematic approach to implementing change. Such approaches have much in common with school development planning, at least in terms of some of the general principles which inform them, though they originated and were developed outside the education system, in large commercial companies such as ICI. One such approach which has been adapted for use in education is known as the systematic management of change (Everard and Morris 1985).

The process of managing change is seen to involve several stages (see Figure 5.2).

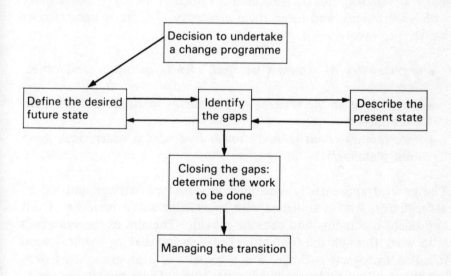

Figure 5.2 The stages of systematic management of change

The assumption in this approach is that managing change is different from day-to-day management and that groups involved in the process of transition management will need to identify the tasks and roles needed to bring about the change. The tasks of gaining the commitment for the change and dealing with resistance are recognised as most significant and various specific methods are available for dealing with these. Further details about these can be found in Evans *et al.* (1989).

Another approach to planning change, which was developed in the context of local government policy making, called the strategic choice approach (Friend and Hickling 1987), has been tried out to explore the possibilities of setting up a cluster arrangement for SEN in one LEA (Evans *et al.* 1989). It is an approach which has relevance to the planning of clusters where representatives from different schools might have different policies and assumptions. In such a situation it may be unrealistic to start, as does the systematic management of change by trying to develop shared objectives. The approach is accordingly concerned more with managing the process of planning rather than setting priorities and targets in advance.

The strategic choice approach focuses on facilitating and guiding the processes of decision-making. Such decision-making is seen to be made under various constraints, such as, the shortage of time, limited resources and limited freedom of manoeuvre. The challenge of decision-making is seen to involve living constructively with uncertainties and using them creatively. The main uncertainties are seen to involve:

- *uncertainties of values* ('we need clearer priorities and objectives');
- *uncertainties in the working environment* ('we need more research, more facts';
- *uncertainties about related choices* ('we need a wider view, more joint planning').

The general approach is used in workshop-type settings and led by a facilitator, who is someone with knowledge and experience of this approach to planning and decision-making. The aim of the workshop is to work through the four modes of decision-making towards what is called a progress package, which consists of a programme of steps towards making and enacting the decisions. These modes are represented in Figure 5.3.

Part of clarifying what activities are involved in a cluster arrangement is deciding how the shared resources will be used. In specifying this as part of the planning, it would also be useful for individual schools to clarify which aspects of their resources for SEN use are *not* part of the shared cluster resource. Doing this is another way of considering

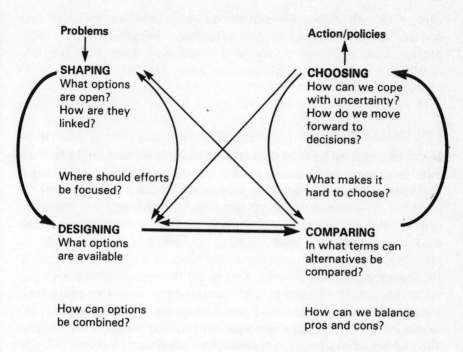

Figure 5.3 The four modes of decision-making in the strategic choice approach

how the SEN inter-school collaboration will be co-ordinated with the individual school's own SEN policy and practice.

Cluster management group

Pooling resources requires some form of inter-school group to manage their allocation and use. This raises important considerations about who will be members of the managing or steering group and what brief this group will have in terms of its formal procedures, areas of responsibilities and activities. Central to this will be the question of how the shared resources will be managed by the group.

Whatever the agreed system, it will be judged in terms of whether the resource allocation will be seen by the participating schools to be fair and to their own benefit over the span of the cluster. This is where principles of mutuality and fair exchange are relevant.

Decisions are also needed about the membership of the group. To record decisions, the participating schools might wish to have a written agreement with each other and the LEA, if involved, to cover such matters as the formality of the procedures, duration of the cluster arrangement, a future review and evaluation date, and even the conditions under which schools can enter and withdraw from the arrangement.

Concluding comments

In this chapter, we have tried to consider how those who might be interested in a cluster development might go about thinking about the matter and how they might proceed to plan an inter-school development. We have not gone into detail about techniques of planning and managing change. For readers who are not too familiar with these, we would recommend that they refer to other sources. Those responsible for planning development activities might wish to invite a consultant to facilitate the planning process. This could be someone either with previous experience of setting up and managing a cluster or an educational consultant with more general know-how about managing change. We would emphasise both the importance of having some outside support and the use of systematic approaches to developing a cluster.

In whatever way it is decided to proceed, it may be useful for any group considering moving towards some form of cluster arrangement to ask themselves the following questions before they start the process of change.

Initiation

- Have the initiators involved other interested individuals and groups in systematic consultation about the cluster plan?
- Has consultation involved a comprehensive and systematic weighing up of the advantages and disadvantages of SEN inter-school collaboration?
- Have the LEA and other service contexts been considered by the initiators?

Goals

- Are there specific goals for the SEN collaboration?
- How are the goals linked to the individual schools' SEN policy and practice?
- Have the goals been discussed and endorsed by those who have

a stake in the arrangements, for example, governors, SEN teachers?

- If the goals of SEN collaboration are part of a wider set of collaboration goals, how are the SEN goals to be maintained while being integrated with the wider goals?

Collaboration activities

- Over what specific activities will the schools in the cluster collaborate?
- If there are a range of collaboration activities, for example, joint INSET and shared SEN support teaching, how are these different activities to be co-ordinated?
- Is there a clear distinction between collaboration which involves exchange between schools (of pupils, teachers, materials) and collaboration which involves joint sharing and managing of resources (of teachers, assistants, materials)?

Size and membership of cluster

- Is collaboration to be between schools of a single phase, for example, primary or secondary, or across phase, for example, secondary with some primaries?
- Is collaboration going to include special school(s) in the arrangement?
- Is location of the collaborating schools important for the arrangement – for example, in terms of travelling distance?
- What is the optimum size of the cluster for the goals of the arrangement?
- Do the individual schools which might join the cluster have prior experience of inter-school collaboration and was it positive?
- If LEAs are initiating clusters, will schools be encouraged to choose their own cluster groups or be directed to form clusters as part of a wider LEA plan?

Resources

- What resources will be shared jointly within the cluster (staff time, materials, funds)?
- Where do the resources come from? (From individual schools

devolved budgets; from LEA's discretionary exempted budget; from devolved Statemented resources; from some combination of above?)

- What specific activities will shared resources be used for and what not for?
- How will the use of the shared cluster resource be co-ordinated with individual schools' SEN policy and practice?

Management group

- How will the shared resources be managed by the cluster schools?
- Will the system of allocating the shared resources be seen by the participating schools to benefit them over the span of the cluster?
- If there will be a steering/management group, who will be members and what procedures will operate?
- What kind of agreement will the participating schools have with each other/LEA about the cluster? (Formality of procedures; duration of cluster arrangement; conditions under which schools can enter/withdraw; evaluation and review date?)

Some materials to help those involved in exploring the idea of a cluster are contained in Appendices A and B.

CHAPTER 6

Conclusions

In this book we have set out to look at clusters of schools as a way of contributing to meeting pupils' SEN. The research on which the book is based was carried out at a time of increasing instability and turbulence within the educational environment, falling as it did between the implementation of the Education Acts of 1988 and 1993. Chapter 1 sets the research in this context and describes some of the aspects of recent legislative and other developments which have affected and continue to affect provision for pupils with special educational needs. Indeed the past decade has been characterised by developments and change in SEN provision. A question highlighted in the more recent period, for example in the report of the Audit Commission/HMI (1992) is over the respective responsibilities of LEAs and schools for pupils with SEN, now further complicated by the setting up of FAS in areas where over 10 per cent of pupils are in grant-maintained schools. The Fish Report (ILEA 1985) recommended clusters of schools taking on responsibility for pupils with SEN in their community: this was an area of interest in the research.

In Chapter 2, we have reviewed some of the literature on collaboration and collaborative linkages in a general sense, including more formal federations and less formal networks. We have looked at some of the problems in the way of collaboration, drawing on a review by Hudson (1987) and at some strategies for achieving collaboration starting with an analysis by Benson (1975). Of particular interest has been the issue of the balance between costs and benefits for schools in collaboration and some of the potential incentives for schools in terms of enhancing the resources available to them.

Chapters 3 and 4 present some of our research findings. The four LEA case studies of clusters revealed collaborative arrangements which were very different in nature. Using interviews in the LEAs with a number of different people, including officers, advisers, educational psychologists, medical officers, headteachers, support teachers, class teachers and pupils, we were able to describe in some detail the origins, the workings and the outcomes of the collaborative arrangements and to begin to consider their effectiveness in contributing to meeting pupils' SEN. We have identified some dimensions and factors in cluster organisation which seem important. The group discussion involving officers, advisers, educational psychologists, headteachers and governors, in twelve further LEAs enabled us to explore other cluster arrangements and to discuss views on the possibility or likelihood of such arrangements in the future.

In Chapter 5 we have set out some practical suggestions for those who might wish to develop arrangements for inter-school collaboration. Drawing on some of the general frameworks for school review and development (for example, GRIDS, Abbot *et al*. 1988) and school development planning (Hargreaves and Hopkins 1991), we look at ways of undertaking a development process. Two of the authors have previously developed relevant materials in the area of decision-making (Evans *et al*. 1989) using the strategic choice approach (Friend and Hickling 1987); this approach is used in our consideration of possible development activities. The appendices offer some suggestions for practical activities related to these considerations.

It is even more difficult to predict development in the current rapid changing educational environment, at a time when substantial legislation is being implemented and detailed circulars of guidance are causing schools and LEAs to reorganise procedures and provision. However, the shift of responsibility and resources for a larger number of pupils with SEN from LEAs back to schools means that it is at the school level that most of the provision will need to be organised. Cluster groupings of schools may provide a means for schools to achieve economies of scale and sharing of expertise which could enhance the abilities of individual schools to provide for pupils with SEN. There is some evidence from the research to support developments in this direction, and it is our hope and belief that collaboration between schools in relation to meeting pupils' SEN will provide a positive way forward in the current educational context.

Appendix A

Some possible development activities

There is no 'one best way' to go about the planning of a cluster arrangement. The approach which we are taking is that there are general principles and a range of planning modes which can be useful. In this appendix, we outline one sequence which can be followed to initiate a cluster fully aware that there are others which may be as good or better. Figure A.1 is a summary of such a sequence. We are going to focus on two important stages in this sequence – the exploratory meeting and the cluster plan formulation activity (marked with an * in the sequence in Figure A.1).

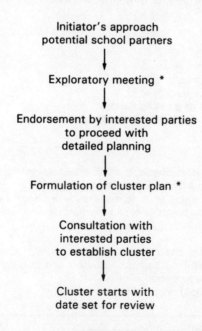

Initiator's approach
potential school partners

↓

Exploratory meeting *

↓

Endorsement by interested parties
to proceed with
detailed planning

↓

Formulation of cluster plan *

↓

Consultation with
interested parties
to establish cluster

↓

Cluster starts with
date set for review

Figure A.1 A sequence of actions to initiate a cluster arrangement

The exploratory meeting

The exploratory meeting can be used as an opportunity to bring together representatives from the different schools which might be interested in forming a cluster. Decisions will need to be made about whether, at this

---

Aims
1. to raise awareness about the nature of inter-school collaboration as a way of enhancing provision for SEN;
2. to enable participants to explore their views about the positive and negative implications of setting up a SEN cluster;
3. to enable the participants to be in a position to consult with others so that a decision can be made whether to proceed to the cluster planning stage or not.

Materials
1. some relevant reading about clusters for SEN – this could be taken from part of this book or from some article about clusters (see References for these);
2. copies of the cluster advantages/disadvantages inventory (see Appendix B).

Pre-reading
Participants at meeting to be sent the cluster reading in advance so they can discuss its content at the meeting.

Possible timing

Session	Activity
1	Introduction: ● to explain aims and programme; ● to provide background.
2	A talk about an existing cluster: ● from someone with experience of a cluster.

BREAK

3	Exercise for participants to think about advantages and disadvantages of setting up a SEN cluster using either: i) a SWOT exercise – to explore participants' views about the strengths, weaknesses, opportunities and threats of a cluster arrangement; or ii) the cluster inventory exercise* – to help participants to consider the possible outcomes of clusters and to weigh up how you think about these overall.
4	Decisions about ways forward.

Figure A.2 Exploratory meeting programme

Note: *see materials in Appendix B

stage, to invite representatives from groups and agencies, other than schools, who may make up the cluster, such as eductional psychology and social services. The main purposes of such a meeting can be seen to include both awareness raising about clusters and enough exploration of what is involved to enable the potential collaborators to seek authorisation about whether to take part in cluster planning. Figure A.2 outlines the aims, activities and possible format of an exploratory meeting.

Two possible activities have been suggested for session 3 in this programme. The SWOT exercise is fairly well known as a general way of structuring the views and evaluations of a group about a particular project or development. The emphasis is on considering both positive and negative aspects in terms of the development itself, but also of circumstances which might support and interfere with the development. The cluster inventory exercise is more specifically focused on the possible outcomes of a cluster. It has been designed in the light of our cluster research findings and enables participants to think through individually what they expect to come of a cluster arrangement and how they evaluate these outcomes. Once participants have completed the inventory they can then share their views with each other in groups.

Meeting to formulate cluster plan

This meeting is likely to involve fewer people than the exploratory meeting as the purpose is to design and record some detailed cluster proposals which can then be shown to a wider group of interested parties. Though there are several ways in which such a meeting can be conducted, its proceedings need to be co-ordinated, either by one person or several people in turn. Some of the systematic approaches to planning and decision-making mentioned in Chapter 5 can be drawn on at a meeting like this.

Appendix B

Inventory for schools to assess the advantages and disadvantages of participating in a cluster arrangement

The purpose of this exercise is to help you think about the advantages and disadvantages of clustering. It has two parts:

1. to help you consider outcomes;
2. to weigh up how you think about these overall. The point of the exercise is to stimulate thinking about whether to plan SENs-related inter-school collaboration.

Part 1

The following statements express some possible outcomes of being part of a scheme of inter-school collaboration for SENs. They express some possible positive and negative outcomes. Read each statement and tick whether you consider each outcome in terms of it being:

	i.	likely – unlikely
and	ii.	positive – negative

REMEMBER TO PUT TWO TICKS IN RESPONSE TO EACH STATEMENT

1. Clustering would enable schools to cope better with pupils having difficulties in learning.

likely	unsure	unlikely	positive	unsure	negative

2. Clustering would enable schools to make fewer requests for statutory assessments and Statements.

| likely | unsure | unlikely | | positive | unsure | negative |

3. Clustering would enable schools to make fewer requests to support services, for example educational psychology services.

| likely | unsure | unlikely | | positive | unsure | negative |

4. Clustering would have a limited impact on the SENs practices in individual schools.

| likely | unsure | unlikely | | positive | unsure | negative |

5. Clustering would involve the school in time-consuming working relationships.

| likely | unsure | unlikely | | positive | unsure | negative |

6. Clustering would increase teachers' confidence and their sense of being supported.

| likely | unsure | unlikely | | positive | unsure | negative |

7. Clustering would stimulate the school to develop and enhance its whole-school SEN policy and practice.

| likely | unsure | unlikely | | positive | unsure | negative |

8. Clustering would enable teachers to adopt new teaching methods and techniques.

___	___	___		___	___	___
likely	unsure	unlikely		positive	unsure	negative

9. Clustering would benefit teachers who were directly involved in collaboration.

___	___	___		___	___	___
likely	unsure	unlikely		positive	unsure	negative

10. Clustering would enable schools to collaborate with schools more widely over other activities.

___	___	___		___	___	___
likely	unsure	unlikely		positive	unsure	negative

11. Clustering would enable schools to feel less isolated and more supported in providing for pupils with SENs.

___	___	___		___	___	___
likely	unsure	unlikely		positive	unsure	negative

12. Clustering would take teachers directly involved in the scheme away from their normal responsibilities, for example from class teaching.

___	___	___		___	___	___
likely	unsure	unlikely		positive	unsure	negative

13. Clustering would involve schools in disagreements and conflicts about managing the collaboration scheme.

___	___	___		___	___	___
likely	unsure	unlikely		positive	unsure	negative

14. Clustering would enable schools to form better working links with health and social support services.

| likely | unsure | unlikely | positive | unsure | negative |

15. Clusters would enable schools to get better value out of their available resources through economies of scale.

| likely | unsure | unlikely | positive | unsure | negative |

Part 2

You have given an initial response for each of the above 15 statements about how likely−unlikely and how positive−negative you see these outcomes.

You can now summarise and get an overview of your views about SEN inter-school collaboration by transferring your two responses for each statement to the grid below.

To do this, write each statement number in one of the nine cells according to your response to its likelihood and to its value.

For example:

● if you rated statement 8 as a likely outcome and as a positive outcome, put 8 in the top left cell − cell 1;
● if you rated statement 13 as an unlikely outcome and you were unsure about its value, put 13 in cell 6.

Summary table:

VALUE	Likely	Unsure	Unlikely
Positive	1	2	3
Unsure	4	5	6
Negative	7	8	9

Interpreting the table

The table shows you the overall distribution of your responses. You may have the numbers distributed evenly across the nine cells or placed mainly in only a few cells.

Here are some pointers to interpreting your overall view:

- if your statement numbers are mainly in cell 1, then this indicates that you see advantages to clustering for SEN.
- if your statement numbers are in the positive row − cells 1, 2 or 3, with most in cells 2 or 3, then this suggests that you value developing SEN policy and practices but have doubts about whether clustering will lead to these positive outcomes;
- if your statements are mainly in the unsure column or row − cells 4, 5, 6, 2 and 8, then this indicates that your are unsure about the value of developing SEN policy and practice and/or whether clustering will lead to these outcomes.

There are, of course, no hard and fast ways of interpreting such an exercise. If the exercise is done by a group of people, then this gives the group a basis for assessing the degree of consensus about a SEN inter-school collaboration initiative. Having analysed the summary table, you might wish to reconsider your initial responses to the likelihood and value of the possible cluster outcomes. If you come to do this, then the exercise was worth doing.

References

Abbott, R., Birchenough, M. and Steadman, S. (1988) *GRIDS: secondary and primary school handbooks.* London: Longman for SCDC.

Aldrich, H.E. (1976) 'Resource dependence and inter-organisational relationships', *Administration and Society,* 8, 419–53.

Aldrich, H.E. (1979) *Organisations and Environments.* Englewood Cliffs NJ: Prentice-Hall.

Audit Commission/HMI (1992) *Getting in on the Act. Provision for pupils with special educational needs: the national picture.* London: HMSO.

Bangs, J. (1993) 'Support services–stability or erosion?', *British Journal of Special Education,* 20, 3, 105–7.

Bell, L. (1980) 'The school as an organisation: a reappraisal', *British Journal of Sociology of Education,* 1, 2, 183–92.

Benford, M. (1988) 'Beyond clustering', *Education,* 23.9.88, 294–5.

Benson, J. (1975) 'The inter-organisational network as political economy', *Administrative Science Quarterly,* 20, 229–49.

Bray, M. (1987) *School Clusters in the Third World.* Paris: Unesco-Unicef.

Corwin, R.G. (1981) 'Patterns of organisational control and teacher militancy: theoretical continuities in the idea of "loose coupling"' *Research in the Sociology of Education and Socialization,* 2, 261–91.

Cowne, E. and Norwich, B. (1987) *Lessons in Partnership.* Bedford Way Papers, University of London Institute of Education.

Davie, R. (1993) 'Implementing Warnock's multi-professional approach', in J. Visser and G. Upton (eds) *Special Education in Britain after Warnock.* London: David Fulton Publishers.

Dearing, R. (1993) *The National Curriculum and its Assessment: an interim report.* National Curriculum Council and Schools Examination and Assessment Council.

Department of Education and Science (1978) *The Warnock Report.* London: HMSO.

Department of Education and Science (1988) *Education Reform Act 1988.* London: HMSO.

Department for Education (1993a) *Education Act 1993.* London: HMSO.

Department for Education (1993b) *Education Act 1993.* Draft Code of Practice on the Identification and Assessment of Special Educational Needs.

Department for Education (1993c) *Education Act 1993.* Draft Circular on the Organisation of Special Educational Provision.

Department for Education (1993d) Draft Circulars on 'Pupils with Problems'.

Department for Education (1994) Circular 2/94 'Local Management of Schools'.

Emery, F. and Trist, E. (1965) 'The causal texture of organisational environments', *Human Relations,* 18, 21–31.

Evans, J., Everard, B., Friend, J., Glaser, A., Norwich, B. and Welton, J. (1989) *Decision-making for Special Educational Needs, an Inter-service Resourcepack.* University of London, Institute of Education.

Evans, J. and Lunt, I. (1992) *Special Educational Needs under LMS.* London: Institute of Education monograph.

Everard, K.B. and Morris, G. (1985) *Effective School Management.* London: Harper and Row.

Fletcher-Campbell, F. and Hall, C. (1993) *LEA Support for Special Educational Needs.* Slough: NFER.

Friend, J and Hickling, A. (1987) *Planning under Pressure: The Strategic Choice Approach.* Oxford: Pergamon Press

Gains, C. (1992) 'Clustering in Kirkby', *Special!* September, 24–6.

Galton, M., Fogelman, K., Hargreaves, L. and Cavendish, S. (1991) *The Rural Schools Curriculum Enhancement National Evaluation (SCENE) Project. Final Report.* London: Department of Education and Science.

Goacher, B., Evans, J., Welton, J. and Wedell, K. (1988) *Policy and Provision for Special Educational Needs.* London: Cassell.

Hall, V. and Wallace, M. (1993) 'Collaboration as a subversive activity: a professional response to externally imposed competition between schools?', *School Organisation*, 13, 2, 101–14.

Hargreaves, D. and Hopkins, D. (1991) *The Empowered School: the management and practice of development planning*. London: Cassell.

Hazenfield, Y. (1972) 'People processing organisations: an exchange approach', *American Sociological Review*, 37, 256–63.

Her Majesty's Inspectors (1989) *A Survey of Pupils with Special Needs in Ordinary Schools*. London: Department of Education and Science.

House of Commons Education Select Committee (1993) *Meeting Special Educational Needs: statements of need and provision*. London: HMSO.

Huberman, A.M. and Miles, M.B. (1984) *Innovation up Close. How school improvement works*. New York and London: Plenum Press.

Hudson, B. (1987) 'Collaboration in social welfare: a framework for analysis', *Policy and Politics*, 15, 3, 175–82.

ILEA (1985) *Educational Opportunities for All? (The Fish Report)*. London: ILEA.

Litwak, E. and Hylton, L. (1962) 'Interorganisational analysis: a hypothesis on co-ordinating agencies', *Administrative Science Quarterly*, 6, 395–420.

Lunt, I. and Evans, J. (1994) *Allocating Resources for Special Educational Needs Provision. Fourth seminar on policy options for special educational needs in the 1990s*. University of London Institute of Education, NASEN.

Morgan, D.L. (1988) *Focus Groups as Qualitative Research*. London: Sage Publications.

Moses, D., Hegarty, S. and Jowett, S. (1988) *Supporting Ordinary Schools: LEA initiatives*. Windsor: NFER-Nelson.

National Commission on Education (1993) *Learning to Succeed. A radical look at education today and a strategy for the future*. London: Heinemann.

Norwich, B. (1992) *Time to Change the 1981 Education Act*. London: Tufnell Press.

Wallace, M. (1988) 'Innovation for all: management development in small primary schools', *Educational Management and Administration*, 16, 15–24.

Wedell, K. (1986) 'Effective Clusters', *Times Educational Supplement*, 19.10.86.

Wedell, K. (1991) 'Special educational provision in the context of legislative changes', in S. Segal and V. Varma (eds) *Prospects for People with Learning Difficulties*. London: David Fulton Publishers.

Wedell, K. (1993a) 'Varieties of school integration', in P. Mittler, R. Brouillette and D. Harris (eds) *World Yearbook of Education: 1993 Special Education*. London: Kogan Page.

Wedell, K. (1993b) 'Special needs education: the next 25 years', in National Commission on Education: *Briefings*. London: Heinemann.

Weick, K.E. (1976) 'Education organisations as loosely-coupled systems', *Administrative Science Quarterly*, 21, 1, 1–19.

Weston, P. and Barrett, E. (1992) *The Quest for Coherence. Managing the whole curriculum 5–16*. Slough: NFER.

Yuchtman, E. and Seashore, S. (1967) 'A system resource approach to organisational effectiveness', *American Sociological Review*, 32, 891–903.

INDEX

Author Index

Subject Index

Special Educational Consortium (SEC) 9
special educational needs (SEN)
  advantages of clusters for
  provision of services 72−3
  allocation of resources for 2−4
  as continuum vii, 2
  definition of 5
  and development planning 77−81
  encouraging collaboration 27−9, 47
  future responsibility for ix
  guideline requirements for schools
    71−2
  nature of provision for 49−50
  social and health services for 75−6, 89
  Statement procedure *see* Statements
special schools and units 5, 49
  inclusion in clusters 27−9, 44
  as resource centres 44
  resources of 2, 3
  and Statement procedure 4
staff development, clusters serving as 38
standardisation in collaborative linkages
    25−6
Statements
  for behaviour problems 64
  procedures for vii, 3−5
  and resource levels 49
  responsibilities for SEN pupils without
    71

rising numbers of 8, 42, 71
and special schools and units 4
variations in rates 5
strategies for collaboration
  authoritative 27
  co-operative 26
  incentives 26−7
support services
  by Local Education Authorities
    (LEAs) 3, 28−9, 71
  provision for 5, 38−40
support teachers, and cluster
    arrangements 75
SWOT exercises 88, 89

teachers
  advantages of clusters for 64−5, 73
  disadvantages of clusters for 63
  work-load increased by
    collaboration 67
  see also headteachers
team leaders, role of 57−8
team leaders *see also* co-ordinators
Technical and Vocational Education
    Initiative (TVEI) viii, 26

whole-school policies for SEN 6, 10
  development planning 77−81